GREAT AMERICAN HOMES

Old New Orleans

BY VANCE MUSE
PHOTOGRAPHY BY KAREN RADKAI

Oxmoor House®

Great American Homes
was created and produced by
Rebus, Inc.
and published by Oxmoor House, Inc.

Rebus, Inc.
Publisher: Rodney Friedman
Editor: Charles L. Mee, Jr.
Picture Editor: Mary Z. Jenkins
Art Director: Ronald Gross
Managing Editor: Fredrica A. Harvey
Consulting Editor: Michael Goldman

Production: Paul Levin,
Giga Communications, Inc.

Author: Vance Muse is a writer at *Life*
magazine. He has also contributed
articles to *House & Garden, Texas
Monthly,* and other publications.

Photographer: Karen Radkai is a
photographer based in New York and
Paris. Her work has appeared in *House
& Garden, World of Interiors, Vogue,* and
Self.

Consultant: Samuel J. Dornsife,
A.S.I.D., F.R.S.A., is a designer and
lecturer specializing in American
decorative arts of the nineteenth
century. He is a special consultant to the
American Wing of the Metropolitan
Museum of Art in New York and has
advised on the restoration of several of
the nation's historic houses.

Published by Oxmoor House, Inc.
Book Division of Southern Progress Corporation
P.O. Box 2463
Birmingham, AL 35201

Library of Congress
Cataloging in Publication Data
Muse, Vance, 1949–
  Old New Orleans.

  (Great American homes)
  Includes index.
  1. New Orleans (La.)—Dwellings.
  2. Historic buildings—Louisiana—New Orleans.
  3. Eclecticism in architecture—Louisiana—New Orleans.
  I. Title. II. Series.
NA7238.N5M8 720'.9763'35 84-15501
ISBN 0-8487-0757-5

Cover: Maddox-Brennan House.

CONTENTS

FOREWORD

JACKSON SQUARE

To a great extent New Orleans looks like the city it was long ago. Certainly the streets of the city have changed, and the things in them, but the remarkable number of buildings surviving from the eighteenth and nineteenth centuries have challenged time. *Old New Orleans* presents a sampling of the city's most significant historic houses, architectural treasures that follow the town's development from a New France trading depot, to a cosmopolitan "New Paris," to the premier antebellum port city.

Concentrated in the Vieux Carré are some of the late-eighteenth-century homes of the Creole descendants of New Orleans' European settlers. Whether four-room cottages or three-story town houses, Creole residences were (and are) ideally suited to the semitropical climate, for they are built in the local French and Spanish Colonial idiom with porte cochere entrances, overhanging roofs and broad galleries, shuttered French doors, and courtyards.

When Americans poured into the city after the Louisiana Purchase in 1803, they brought more formal architectural styles with them. Federal and Georgian houses began to appear, and in the flush decades before the Civil War, the Americans built in the classical revival styles sweeping the country. The Greek Revival and, later, the Italianate styles were particularly popular in New Orleans. Though these houses brought a new look to New Orleans, and different floor plans (with central and side hallways rather than porte cocheres), they were obviously influenced by their Creole forebears. The more elaborate of New Orleans homes, Creole and American alike, were graced with cast iron—the structural and decorative element that has become a virtual symbol of the city. The idea in New Orleans was to strike balances between formality and informality. "Living well" did not mean merely surrounding oneself with expensive possessions, for the greatest luxury of all was to be comfortable on a hot summer day.

New Orleans' historic houses exist today only because individuals and foundations have cared and worked to restore and preserve them. Some of the most important of the city's early historic houses are open to the public as museums; many more are private homes, whose owners have preserved the integrity of the houses' original design and decoration. Outstanding examples of New Orleans' architectural heritage are presented here, in the houses of *Old New Orleans*. This is a story not only of Creoles and Americans but of many peoples, cultures, and influences that have made New Orleans the unique city it is.

SAMUEL WILSON, JR., F.A.I.A.
NEW ORLEANS, LOUISIANA

INTRODUCTION

Though many people are so taken with the old-world charms of New Orleans that they think of the place as some sort of theme park, it is a real city. As real cities do, New Orleans contradicts itself—it is both beautiful and not, and its elegance can be the shabby kind. The city is at once Catholic, heathen, gritty, and grand. It is a city of ancient social hierarchies, of invitation-only balls and members-only clubs, yet the best parties are unseemly free-for-alls on the street. New Orleans is not the city it once was, no longer the magnet of the South, but it has something its rivals lack, something all colorful (or corrupt) characters have: New Orleans has a visible history, a past that is very much present.

Walk the streets and ride the streetcars of New Orleans and you sense the influence of three centuries and more countries. The mixture of cultures—particularly the Creole, of European descent—is evident in the language, cuisine, music, the pace of the city, and in the architectural crossbreeds that define this distinctive cityscape. ("Creole," often thought to be of French origin, is from the Spanish *criar*, to "create" or "breed." The word properly describes the people descended from European colonists and their culture.) While New Orleans looks like no other place, it seems familiar, triggering déjà vu: you might have seen these houses, or parts of them, in the West Indies, or Spain, the south of France, along the eastern seaboard, or on southern plantations. From spare cottages and bungalows to trim town houses and structures that recall Olympus, these historic houses evoke a time when New Orleans was the busiest port in the nation and the richest of cities.

A bed of azaleas is matched, flower for flower it seems, by a cast-iron trellis that forms the front porch and gallery of this Italianate house in New Orleans. The high-spirited decoration over the more formal classical design typifies the relaxed elegance of the city's architecture.

With its modern skyline and Superdome safely in the business district, New Orleans keeps the narrow, sunny streets of the Vieux Carré and the shady avenues of the Garden District much as they were long ago.

Simple to grand, New Orleans' houses are all of a piece, reflecting standards set early in the eighteenth century. A few of the earliest structures stand, survivors of time and of two fires that destroyed most everything else in New Orleans—first in 1788, again in 1794. When not single storied, these handsome cottages follow a provincial European plan with residential quarters above first-floor offices or shops. Oversize roofs top them like wide-brimmed hats, deflecting intense sun and rain, and several pairs of French doors can be completely shuttered—again, against the elements. Though they sit close to the street on the banquette (the French term for "sidewalk" still holds), the cottages are perfectly contained, with their modest facades and shuttered doors. A discreet entrance also ensures privacy: there being no front door, you open a gate at one side of the house, close it behind you, and follow a porte cochere to a courtyard around back. Inside they are cottagey—four rooms square, a layout repeated on additional floors. Front and back rooms join to make simple double parlors, while the others serve as libraries, dining rooms, or bedrooms. The cottages are much

The American flag is raised above New Orleans to celebrate the 1803 Louisiana Purchase, by which France sold the city— and the Territory—to America.

more open than they seem to be from the outside, and they merge quite naturally with the environment. Light comes in through the louvered shutters, and breezes circulate from door to door, cooling the high-ceilinged rooms. Many of those doorways lead to courtyards, balconies, porches, and verandas (also known as galleries), erasing the lines between indoors and out. Airiness is perhaps the most characteristic aspect of New Orleans domestic architecture—one or two alfresco retreats will grace even the smallest cottage, giving it a bivouac quality. Yet these open houses remain remarkably private. Courtyards are hardly visible from the banquettes— you get only a glimpse of green down a walkway or over a rooftop. Adjacent to the courtyard of a more elaborate house will be a *garçonnière,* housing the sons of a large Creole family. (The name is derived from *garçon,* the French for "young man.") Servants' quarters were also located in back, as were kitchens—Creoles isolated their hearths and ovens to confine heat and check fire. This, in tropical New Orleans, was essentially the mold for houses, a plan devised to cope with heat and stormy weather and to maximize passing breezes and garden delights. (Fireplaces do nicely on the occasions when New Orleans is chilly.)

As the city grew the architecture became more eclectic, even eccentric, a perfect backdrop for a gay and rich society. Creoles showed little restraint in their hybrid houses, juxtaposing styles and dressing up the places with baroque twists of wrought iron. Entire galleries and balconies of cast iron, already exuberant for their floral forms, were painted bright colors. Also popular were *faux* effects, elements of make-believe that relieved a wanting landscape. Creoles treated plain stucco facades to resemble ashlar, granite, and marble. Rough-grained woods were disguised as something finer, baseboards were marbleized. Though not ostentatious, wealthy Creoles did not skimp on their surroundings, appointing their large rooms with imported furniture, porcelain, crystal. Physical comfort, though, was always the first priority and toward that, even the most gussied-up house retained elements of the early cottage. Few would suffer— or risk—a kitchen in the main house. No one could do without high ceilings and many French doors, positioned for cross ventilation and shuttered. And whatever their

Andrew Jackson, who saved New Orleans from the British in the War of 1812, is commemorated by a bronze statue in the square that bears his name.

means the Creoles considered courtyards, balconies, and galleries not luxuries but essentials—for theirs was a difficult environment.

New Orleans lies below sea level in what was once a cypress swamp, and before a single cottage could be built, some solidity had to be imparted into the land. Levees were raised, and oyster shells were used as landfill. Still, the swamp was not easily tamed and by all early accounts, the colonists' chief rivals for the site were alligators and water moccasins. No foundation could be dug, nor any grave—water seeped into houses not raised off the ground, and a six-foot burial was unthinkable. (The great old cemeteries of New Orleans, with their above-ground tombs in ruin, are a chilling architectural legacy.) Water was, and is, everywhere: the Mississippi River cuts one convoluted border line, and Lake Pontchartrain closes off the other side of the city. In between and down below these bodies of water is New Orleans, shot through with bayous and waiting to be engulfed from either direction. South and west of the city, toward the Gulf of Mexico, is swampland (including the regions settled by French Acadians, whose descendants are known as Cajuns). Though inland, New Orleans can be as inclement as any coastal town. Hurricanes tear in from the Gulf, the area's rainstorms are rarely moderate, and the summer sun burns into the fall. The intense heat and wetness collude of course, and the humidity descending on New Orleans is of a kind that only a mosquito or an orchid could love.

The area did not provide the best building materials—there were no quarries of marble or granite, no great hardwood forests. But there were acres of cypress trees, and their tall timbers are practically resistant to rot-

This early cottage on Bourbon Street is known as Laffite's Blacksmith Shop—the French pirate Jean Laffite allegedly used it as a cover for smuggling operations. The stucco has eroded, exposing the standard brick-between-posts construction.

ting. Magnolia and cedar were also available, pine and walnut, too, but none so abundantly as cypress; it is hard to find an old house in New Orleans not constructed and even trimmed with this native wood. Cypress was crucial not just for the framework of a house, but also to strengthen bricks, which were made with squishy local clay. The bricks were laid between vertical and diagonal cypress posts in a unique construction the French called *briquette-entre-poteaux*—"brick between posts." The crumbly bricks needed further protection, and repeated smearings of stucco made a sturdy house, and a cool one. Occasionally you find a patch of wall, its stucco veneer worn away, exposing *briquette-entre-poteaux* that is more than two hundred years old. Seeing under the surface you can appreciate the achievement of the men and women whose task it was to build New Orleans. Of them all it was the French, even when outnumbered and overpowered, who dominated the style of the city and gave it its lasting character.

New Orleans did not exist until 1718, when the French explorer Sieur de Bienville set off to establish a trading center for France's Colonial empire. A natural gulf port did not exist—at least not one easily negotiated—so Bienville pushed up the Mississippi nearly one hundred miles to the great bend in the river that now marks the very locus of the Vieux Carré. Somehow undiscouraged by the fact that he and his men stepped onto land that was anything but dry, Bienville claimed the oozy spot as Nouvelle Orléans, after Philippe II d'Orléans, the powerful regent of Louis XV. The regent was a scandal throughout Europe—for his orgies, which he threw even on Good Friday, and for his drinking, which eventually killed him. (It seems that his behavior was forgivable: Voltaire wrote that the regent's only faults were "too much love of pleasure, too much love of novelty.") It is perhaps appropriate that what is generally regarded as America's most intemperate and wicked city should be named after such a rake.

France did not think much of New Orleans and, except to tap its (mostly unforeseen) wealth, largely left the colony to explorers and crews of adventurers and traders. Much of the labor in the colony was provided by ex-convicts, freed from French prisons just for that purpose. To accommodate the young men, the monarchy dispatched a shipload of orphan girls and, to mind them prior to their marriages, a few Jesuit priests and a contingent of Ursuline nuns. (The Ursuline Convent, built in 1727 and rebuilt after a fire in 1745, is the oldest structure in the Mississippi River valley.) To draw more people to the ragtag colony, the king enlisted John Law, who would be described today as a promoter. Law pitched "New France" as a paradise and many fell for the real estate scam, sailing off to the swamp: among the arrivals were giddy fortune seekers, nobles who had lost their estates, and peasants who had nothing to lose. From the West Indies came other Frenchmen, and Spaniards, with their slaves. And there were pirates, including Jean Laffite. Together they would build a city that would require no forced settlement but would attract, on its own merits, a bright and ambitious population.

They began at Bienville's bend in the river, by marking out a walled gridiron of streets. The plan was French in its formality, and there is no mistaking its origin: there is a Toulouse Street, and a Conti, Chartres, Dauphine, Orleans, Bourbon.

These little white cottages, discreetly shuttered, were most likely homes of femmes de couleur libre, *the quadroon mistresses of Creole gentlemen. In this 1844 watercolor one woman leaves her cottage as a neighbor returns.*

Some of the intersecting streets in the Catholic city honor saints: Ann, Peter, Phillip, Louis. The "Old Square," or Vieux Carré (more familiarly known today as the French Quarter), was the extent of New Orleans until later in the eighteenth century when the Creoles developed faubourgs, or suburbs. Though France lost New Orleans in a 1762 treaty with Spain, the city remained overridingly French—in attitude, in the language of the street, and in architecture. (There are architectural gestures that seem impish: after the Spanish built their majestic Cabildo statehouse and presbytère on either side of St. Louis Cathedral, French patrons added to the structures mansard roofs, blatantly Gallic.) The people got along, however, and intermarried, making the Creole culture. Revolu-

In low-lying New Orleans most graves were above ground. All Saints' Day—November 1—was a festive occasion to decorate the tombs of loved ones, as in this 1885 engraving.

tions in France and the West Indies brought royalist refugees to New Orleans, courtly characters who must have longed for the gardens of Versailles as they sloshed through their adopted streets. Comparatively low on pomp, New Orleans did offer more to these aristocrats than they expected: there were several theaters, three opera houses, ballrooms, the elegant residences. And there were fine furnishings, from France at that. A wealthy man could buy all the slaves he wanted. A special class of blacks emerged in New Orleans, too, the *gens de couleur libre*, or "free people of color," who built in the Vieux Carré, mixed in Creole society, and owned slaves themselves.

France briefly reassumed the colony in 1803, and when the United States made the Louisiana Purchase later that year the Creoles were stunned to find themselves living in an American boomtown. A port for both river and gulf, New Orleans linked the South to the Midwest and East and brought in spectacular ocean commerce. It seemed all you had to do was stick out your hand to strike it rich—in the slave trade, or in cotton, sugar, rice, or shipping. Steamboats arrived and jammed the docks alongside the oceangoing schooners. The increasingly sophisticated city provided a great market for fine merchandise: there were Persian and Turkish rugs, Italian marble, fur pelts, silk from China, casks of French wine and jars of Greek olive oil, coffee from Martinique, furniture from Paris, London, Philadelphia, and New York. A German traveler arrived in New Orleans in 1826 and noted his surprise: "New Orleans, the wet grave... for eighty years the wretched asylum for the outcasts of France and Spain, who could not venture one hundred paces beyond its gates without utterly sinking to the breast in mud…has become in the space of twenty-three years one of the most beautiful cities in the Union, inhabited by 40,000 persons who trade with half the world." Everyone came to the mecca on the Mississippi: not just from France and Spain and the Caribbean islands but Ireland, England, Italy, Germany. Mostly the immigrants were Americans—from other parts of the South, the Midwest, and the East. Frederick Law Olmsted, the New England landscape architect, visited New Orleans and wrote to a friend: "What I have met with [here] has been mainly from Northern people and English."

Schooners and steamboats make their way along the Mississippi River, the source of New Orleans' wealth. By the time this painting was made, about 1840, the city had spread far beyond its original site—the Vieux Carré, or French Quarter.

Americans arrived in numbers jarring to the Creoles, and by the 1830s the two cultures had clashed in a confrontation of new ways with old, the upstart with the established. Turned away from the Vieux Carré, the Americans created their own world uptown, with Canal Street as the dividing line. (Creoles and Americans met to do business there, referring to the street's median as the neutral ground, a designation that persists to this day.) Not at all playful, the antagonism resulted in duels and in the more civilized resolution of establishing, temporarily, separate municipalities.

If New Orleans was already a vision, the unwelcome newcomers enhanced it further when they began to develop the old plantation estates off St. Charles Avenue. They built on large lots, on a large scale, and with grandeur in mind: there were Italianate villas, spired Victorian houses, and edifices in the Gothic Revival style. The antebellum glory of New Orleans, though, is best conveyed in the Greek Revival. (The pretension to things ancient Greek—the mythic gods and heroes, the democratic ideal—was fairly complete: uptown developers named nine streets after the muses.) They called their neighborhood the Garden District and living there was not like living in the Vieux Carré, for Garden District houses were more like those on plantations—some were in fact the in-town residences of planters who had much bigger spreads up the river. Wealthy men built them for show, and there is a formality about the houses that is hard to find even in the most extravagant Creole town house. The formality may be obvious, in great hallways, staircases, and

13

ballrooms. Or it may be subtle, as in the precise arrangement of perfectly appointed parlors, rooms where you do not casually put up your feet. Where Creole houses are relaxed, their American counterparts enforce convention: those dramatic staircases, for instance, do not invite anyone up—they are reserved for the swooping greeting of a hostess or a debutante's descent. French doors and casement windows do open the houses, and, with refreshing informality, people moved furniture onto verandas to make summertime sitting rooms and sleeping porches above the neat gardens. Order reigned on the lawns, too, for this neighborhood got its name not from casual courtyards but from carefully landscaped gardens, all sculpted hedges and geometric flower beds. Where the Creoles had little iron fountains and settees, the Americans furnished elegant pavilions—their gardens, ironically, could be those of French nobility.

As hard as these houses try to look like Greek temples, they finally give in to the prevailing merriment of New Orleans. You see it in their irresistible outdoor accommodations. You even see it on the mighty facades where playful squiggles of cast iron link Corinthian and Ionic columns; making no architectural sense, the ornament seems a nod to the city's Creole spirit. More apparent in the Greek Revival

Jockeys drive their horses from the starting line at a New Orleans racetrack. This scene was a familiar one by the 1840s, when the city was the racing center of the nation. Those cheering in the stands probably had much at stake, for Creoles were famous gamblers.

were the builders' ambitions and what many believed to be New Orleans' future. One local booster expressed this in 1849: "The only rival New Orleans can have...is New York [but we are] destined to be much greater. As Athens molded Greece, and Greece Europe, so this city will influence...the whole American continent."

There was less hyperbole than prophecy in those words, for New Orleans did grow and before the Civil War ranked with the largest cities in the nation. Cosmopolitan visitors found that New Orleans lacked nothing materially or culturally, and no one could fail to note its appearance—the letters of a British society lady praise the city's "old continental aspect" and the "houses with queerly shaped, high roofs and iron balconies...looking deliciously cool for summer use." To the eminent English architect Benjamin Latrobe, New Orleans was "very imposing and handsome." The city was in full swing, and its citizens had no doubts about how to live well nor any hesitation to do so. Not even the war could break its stride: Union troops seized New Orleans early, in 1862, with minimal upset to the economy. For the duration of the war,

A Sunday-best crowd turns out for May Day, 1863—celebrating even though the city is occupied by Union troops. This engraving is from Harper's Weekly.

Union general Benjamin Franklin Butler and his lieutenants occupied some of the city's finest private residences. (The displaced owners tolerated the Yankees and reclaimed their houses after the war.) New Orleans might have prospered even in a devastated South had it not been for another blow, this one technological. By the end of the 1860s, railroads were crossing the country, and the great port on the Mississippi, bypassed, began to lose its economic base. Unable for many years to replace its eighteenth- and nineteenth-century buildings with more modern structures, New Orleans has survived with its historic grandeur intact.

1
PITOT HOUSE
CREOLE COMFORTS

The simple white house could be at home on a tropical island, all crashing waves and swaying palms. Like a bungalow in the West Indies, it springs from its environment, taking advantage of good weather, shutting out bad. Breezes come and go through dozens of tall shuttered windows and French doors, and on pretty days sunlight floods airy rooms. Though delicate in appearance with its skinny second-story columns, called "colonnettes," high hat of a roof, and stucco icing, the house has stood up to withering heat and practically anything blowing in from the Gulf of Mexico. From its raised foundation to its steeply pitched roof, the house perfectly matches New Orleans' tropical climate. That distinctive roof would have made sense in a rain forest or desert; an umbrella and a parasol, it deflects torrential rains and the beating sun.

To live in the house was to live outside of it as well, for the rooms join indoors to outdoors, each opening onto a generous porch, the loggia, or a wide gallery upstairs. Beyond there are only sky, trees, and Bayou St. John. Snaking in from Lake Pontchartrain, the crystalline bayou was once a short carriage ride from town and a sight for city folk's eyes; a contemporary observer wrote that the bayou "charms home-seekers.... The sky may not be bluer overhead there, foliage may not be greener, flowers not bloom more spontaneously—but they seem so to the denizens." To those

Opposite: Pitot House, tucked under its overhanging roof, recalls the simple styles of West Indian plantation houses, which made sense in steamy New Orleans. Architect-builder Hilaire Boutté designed the house about 1799 for the maternal great-grandmother of the French artist Edgar Degas.

Overleaf: Sturdy columns cast shadows across the deep porch; sunlight does not strike the walls. The ceiling is painted grand rouge, *a color mixed from brick dust and buttermilk. The shutters are forest-green, another shade favored by Creoles. The bricks continue into the interior ground floor.*

familiar with the tempestuous West Indies, the house on the bayou seemed to hail from a wilder, windier setting. To James Pitot, one of the city's early entrepreneurs, it looked just right—as if it had blown in on some Caribbean hurricane.

Turbulence of another kind brought James Pitot to New Orleans, for he was twice a refugee from revolutions. As a young Norman named Jacques, Pitot sailed about 1782 to Saint Domingue (now Haiti), the French West Indian colony in the Caribbean, to supervise a brisk trade between wealthy coffee, indigo, and sugar planters and their customers in Europe and the United States. Pitot found his place

James Pitot came to America from Normandy by way of Saint Domingue. This miniature shows Pitot, New Orleans' first elected mayor, in his French finery.

among the Creoles on the island and no doubt enjoyed the high life during his ten years in the exotic Caribbean port city—there were parties, good French theaters, travels to France and nearby islands. But the charm broke with political and social upheavals in two hemispheres—in France, where revolutionaries attacked the monarchy of Louis XVI, and in Saint Domingue, where slave rebellions ended the planters' livelihoods. Pitot saw the horrors of the French Revolution firsthand when, on business in Paris in 1792, he watched a crowd rally round the impaled head of Princess Lamballe, the friend and supporter of the queen, Marie Antoinette. Pitot later found the insurrections in Saint Domingue as threatening: representing the wealthy planters—the slaves' oppressors—he was an enemy of that revolution. Pitot fled to America, settling in Philadelphia where he changed his name to James (perhaps to expedite his acceptance in business circles) and married Marie-Jeanne Marty, who had also fled the uprisings in Saint Domingue. Shortly after their wedding the Pitots made their way to New Orleans where they took to the French Quarter like homesick Frenchmen. At thirty-five James felt he had arrived at the right place at the right time: "[In] a territory almost as vast as all of Europe," he later wrote, "one's imagination can run wild…thinking about the…future promises."

The Pitots were not the only survivors of the revolutions who turned up in New Orleans—the Gallic city attracted many from France and the West Indies, a veritable society of the ancien régime, the crushed royal system. Diehards, these newcomers did not let go of their distinctly French ways. Some claimed to have witnessed horrible scenes at the guillotine and swore they had known the king and queen intimately; they would bide their time in New Orleans, exiles until the monarchy was restored. Royalist sympathy, though, was not unanimous in New Orleans—there were Frenchmen there who supported the revolutionaries back home and later cheered Napoleon Bonaparte.

From his Royal Street town house, Pitot started an import-export business, bringing to the city's markets fine French oak furniture, Madeira, Burgundy, and claret, English silver, porcelain from Paris. To Europe he delivered sugar, cotton, indigo, South American coffee. Established in the business community, Pitot turned some attention to Louisiana's political matters, for the Spanish Colonial government and the local economy (which had not yet begun to soar) troubled him. Pitot frankly did not like the Spaniards and worried that Louisiana (and his own business interests) would stagnate under what he considered their lackadaisical rule. Pitot went so far as to set down his criticisms in a manuscript, *Observations on the Colony of Louisiana*, hoping to influence the French or United States government should either succeed Spain as the possessor of Louisiana. In his *Observations* Pitot blamed the colony's sluggishness on the Spaniards, charging their regime with neglect and corruption. The document seems to have helped Pitot's cause, for when the United States did acquire Louisiana with the famous purchase of 1803 (buying it from France, which had briefly reassumed the colony), W.C.C. Claiborne, governor of the territory, appointed James to the city council, which in turn elected him mayor of New Orleans.

By all accounts Pitot took quick charge of the newly American city: he established a mounted patrol for the rowdy sections of town, opened ferry services on the Mississippi, improved the hospital, built city schools. New Orleans' dirt streets were a hazard and a mess, and Pitot put pavers to work. One of his last acts as mayor, in 1805, was to order a census, which showed a total population, black and white, of 8,475. After less than two years in office, Mayor Pitot resigned, to return to his business. Now with three children—Marie-Odile, Armand-François, and Marie-Jeanne—and well set financially, Pitot began to fancy the life of a country gentleman and looked for a place on Bayou St. John. When he spotted the house—so like the ones he and Marie-Jeanne had known in the West Indies—he snapped it up, along

---

Overleaf: A cypress punkah, an early ceiling fan, stirs air about the dining room, open to the side porch. The mahogany table, made locally about 1820, is ready for tea. Taken from the open pine cupboard is a casual setting of gold-and-white Chinese export porcelain, popular in the early 1800s.

with thirty acres of land. In its bayou setting Pitot's house appealed to bucolic sensibilities but did not isolate the family from the spectacle of the city's commerce: the view included not only earth and sky but schooners and flatboats heaped with cargo.

A veteran of fifteen sultry Louisiana summers, Pitot found much to appreciate about the house, from its *briquette-entre-poteaux* construction to its window-through-window crosscurrents. The seasoned builders of Pitot's house wisely laid brick floors throughout the first level, which cooled the house as if they were marble. Less elegant than the cypress planks upstairs, the bricks did nicely in these rooms given over to work, storage, deliveries, and dining. And if the floor, however highly polished, seemed a bit casual for a dining room, a densely patterned Turkish rug, rolled out beneath a mahogany table set with blue faience and silver candelabra, brought a bit of formality to the scene.

Louisiana Indians Walking Along a Bayou *shows how the Bayou St. John looked—wooded and wild—before European immigrants built houses along its banks. Parisian artist Alfred Boisseau painted this Choctaw family while visiting Louisiana in 1847.*

The riveting feature of the dining room, though, was not any piece of porcelain or silver, but the punkah suspended above the table. A maharaja's ceiling fan, the punkah in Louisiana came to be called a shoofly, for shooing away flies is just what the contraption did. Throughout dinner one of Pitot's younger servants stood in a corner of the room operating the punkah's cords to scatter flies—and, incidentally, stir up a cooling breeze. Despite the prosaic purposes of the combination fly chaser and fan, Pitot's punkah was a local artisan's masterpiece, with French paper filling its cypress frame and a trim of cotton fringe.

Opposite: Cool as a basement but sunny as an attic, Pitot's reception room was also his office. The furniture, including the rocker with its rush seat, was all made in Louisiana in the eighteenth century. On the mantel is English pewter; above it is a portrait of George Washington.

Overleaf: Sun streams into the upstairs drawing room. Notable among the eighteenth-century Louisiana furnishings are the occasional table of mahogany with cabriole legs of cherry and the child's rush-bottomed chair. On the right is a leather "campeachy" chair, derived from a type made in Campeche, Mexico.

A local artist, J.L. Bouqueto de Woiseri, painted the auspicious arrival to New Orleans of a banner-carrying eagle. This panorama from a downriver plantation takes in the long levees, blocks of raised houses, and a wooded area beyond.

Servants Lucille, Miranda, and Nancy shared washing and cleaning chores and each morning brought to the kitchen and loggia in back of the house the garden's herbs and vegetables, piling them on a simple harvest table. Some of the pickings went toward that day's meals, while others were dried, to be stored in an oak pantry. The loggia was as inviting as any room inside the house, with the herbs drying in bunches, flowers thriving in terra-cotta pots and wooden tubs, copper pans hanging from beams, scattered baskets, a singing caged bird. The loggia was painted *grand rouge*, a favorite with Creoles both rich and poor, who made the pigment by mixing brick dust with buttermilk. (*Grand rouge* was not as bold as the name, "big red," implies, and most surfaces in the house were muted: the Pitots painted the beamed ceilings putty-green, a soft grayish color popular through the early nineteenth century. White stucco covered all walls.) On particularly hot days, when even the punkah could not stir the air, the Pitots ate out on the loggia, its open side facing the family's gardens and orchards. The house's single stairway, on the loggia, led to the second-floor enclosed gallery, a summertime sleeping porch. The gallery also served as the upstairs hallway, providing access to the three bedrooms and, through two pairs of tall French doors, the parlor.

In 1813 Governor Claiborne named Pitot to the local judiciary, a lifelong appointment that capped his career. James and Marie-Jeanne apparently made their home a retreat for the writers and politicians they knew, and they entertained visiting dignitaries. (General Victor Moreau, a popular rival of Napoleon's, began his exile from France at the Pitot house.) Considering his company Pitot could take some pride in his achievement, for he had created in his comfortable rooms overlooking the bayou something similar to the salons he had known in France.

Sadness intervened about this time, too, when Marie-Jeanne died giving birth

An upstairs bedroom, open to the bayou, is dominated by a tall-post bed of curly maple (circa 1810), draped and spread with linen and lace. The canopy is called a mosquitaire, for it protects the sleeper from mosquitoes—bringers of yellow fever. The netting also lightens the room during the summer.

to twins. Neither child survived. James eventually met another Creole from Saint Domingue, Genevieve-Sophie Nicolas, and married her in 1816. She and James had two children, Sophie-Gabrielle-Marie and Henri-François, both born on the bayou. The couple chose the parlor, a breezeway of a room, for formal entertaining; it was here before the fireplace that they received guests and retired with them after dinner downstairs. The elaborately carved fireplace mantle was by far the grandest thing in the parlor, actually in the entire house. Though Pitot imported a few treasures (including a beautiful French piano he presented as a belated wedding present to Genevieve-Sophie), he favored furniture in the Federal style, America's

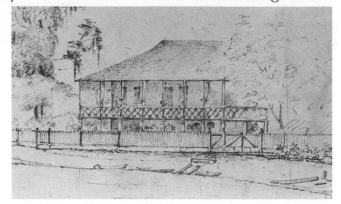

Pitot House, on its original thirty-acre bayou site, makes a tropical scene in this sketch from the 1830s. Then, as now, a picket fence encloses the house, a hip-roofed structure that resembles the plantation homes Pitot had known in the French island colonies.

answer to the new European classicism sparked by the excavations at Pompeii late in the eighteenth century. Where in the neoclassical style an urn or lyre might recall antiquity and celebrate Greek and Roman ideals, flourishes on Federal pieces heralded American independence (a vigilant eagle, the national symbol, was common). Louisiana cabinetmakers excelled at the stately Federal style, and their chairs, tables, and armoires — in native walnut, wild cherry, pine, cypress, and imported mahogany—perfectly suited Pitot's understated rooms. Creoles and Frenchmen did not always appreciate the local woods, however rich the hue, and treated them to resemble European ones. Unhappy with a plain cypress armoire in the master bedroom, Pitot stained it red to look like a cherry closet he had left behind in France. One of the finest pieces in the house was a low table of cherry, cypress, and Saint Domingue mahogany, the rich East Indian wood an imported luxury not everyone could afford. The table was a prize, for its three woods were rarely combined and only by certain cabinetmakers in New Orleans and Charleston.

What made the parlor and bedrooms particularly wonderful to the family was their access to the enormous gallery that surrounded the second floor and seemed to reach clear to the bayou. Out on the gallery playing with his little tin soldiers (an even littler Napoleon leading the toy army), Armand might imagine he was in a tree house. The many French doors, open to breezes and sunlight, encouraged movement from the house to the gallery, from inside to outside. Shutters, louvered to filter harsh sun, could be closed over every door and window in the house; but the environment was never totally shut out: through the louvers, the Pitots could still feel and hear the wind, and smell the rain.

Returning to the city was probably the last thing on Pitot's mind, but in 1819 financial reverses forced him to sell his country estate. From the family's new house, this one on Bourbon Street, Pitot stayed active in the judiciary until his death in 1831. Though he left no such record, it would not be surprising if Pitot looked back with some longing on his decade in that simple tropical house on the bayou. From the din of the Vieux Carré, it must have seemed like paradise.

Overleaf: The loggia is as much a room as any other and, excepting a few cold weeks, a year-round working space. The day's pickings from the garden, and fruit from the French market, went onto the pine harvest table. An open-air dining room, the loggia offers a view of the gardens.

IRON FANCIES

Wrought and cast iron, beautiful in an almost theatrical way, virtually defines New Orleans. In the Vieux Carré and the Garden District, the abundance of the decoration is striking: everywhere are window grilles, fences, balcony railings, entire galleries of iron—in forms of organic and geometric exuberance. In the city's courtyards there are iron fountains and, around them, iron furniture—tables and chairs that are nothing but fanciful tangles of steely vines. In New Orleans even hardware is prettier than it need be: rivets are not simply rivets but rosettes, sunbursts, fleurs-de-lis. The medium has the compelling quality of melding opposites, being at once strong and delicate, masculine and feminine: "iron lace" is the immortal metaphor. The earliest ironwork in New Orleans was wrought at anvils by artisans, most of them blacks, Germans, and Irishmen. By the mid-nineteenth century, local foundries were creating decorative cast iron by pouring molten metal into extravagantly carved wooden molds. Balcony railings, fences, column capitals, and other elements were also available from Philadelphia and New York foundries, whose catalogs listed hundreds of patterns. People of the most discriminating tastes commissioned custom ironwork, featuring favorite motifs—hearts, stars, arrows, flowers, and vines—or family crests. To have one's initials intertwined in an already florid balcony railing or gate was surely the most prestigious of monograms.

Cast-iron gates, framed by Corinthian columns, protect the entrance to Gallier House, built by James Gallier, Jr. in 1857. Delicate in appearance, the pair make a formidable barrier. In New Orleans, architectural ironwork—made locally and in Philadelphia and New York—was popular until the late nineteenth century.

The gate of the Ursuline Convent, circa 1745, bears what are among the oldest wrought-iron ornaments in the Mississippi River valley. Beneath the cross is a grille, through which callers could be scrutinized.

Ironworker Marcellino Hernandez fashioned this unique balcony railing in 1795 for the Chartres Street house of a Spaniard named Bartholeme Bosque: the artist wove his client's initials into the baroque scrollwork.

Flowering iron vines cast their shadows inside a shuttered gallery. Iron galleries such as this one were often added to existing houses, of any style. The frilly ironwork is at home here even on a stately exterior.

The plain border of a Vieux Carré gate, here in detail, gives way to a rich center of fruits and flowers and rococo curls. The gate closes a lush courtyard to passersby.

A scrim of white cast iron turns a grand house into a summer pavilion—it is refreshing even to look at the lacy, arched framework of iron. Palmetto fans and spears alternate in the fence surrounding the property.

A nymph dances around the balcony of an Esplanade Avenue mansion built in 1856 by a prosperous merchant. Each nymph in the railing is framed by a tangle of grapevines, suggesting bacchanalian revelry.

The ornament on this iron fence is spare, but its message is clear: the anvil, hammer, and tongs mark the site of an 1864 ironworks. At this foundry local artisans wrought some of New Orleans' finest ironwork.

Iron grapevines crawl up and about the front of a brick Creole town house in the Vieux Carré. The grape arbor—really a gallery overlooking the street—is of silvery cast iron.

The cornstalk fence—in one of the most exuberant, and the most famous, of New Orleans' cast-iron patterns—surrounds an Italianate house in the Garden District. The fence and gate are composed simply of iron stalks of corn, ready for harvest it seems; in the detail opposite, azaleas mingle with the corn. There are only two such fences in the city—the other is on Royal Street in the Vieux Carré.

2
HERMANN-GRIMA HOUSE
AN AMERICAN LOOK

The host apparently had promised a fireworks display, a typically flamboyant touch by Samuel Hermann, whose new mansion on St. Louis Street was the scene of some of the most extravagant entertainments in New Orleans. A Jewish immigrant from a small town near Frankfort, Germany, Hermann had arrived in Louisiana about 1804 with little else than the impulse to exploit a boomtown. Now, thirty years later, he was one of the city's millionaires, with a house to match his expansive spirit. It seems that Hermann had planned a courtyard party for a breezy March evening, but, just as servants were lighting lanterns, the capricious skies of southern Louisiana darkened. No downpour discouraged Hermann, though, who could simply order the party indoors, having no worry that his rooms would accommodate everyone. Hermann's parties apparently were not to be missed, and even through the storm more than three hundred guests came. One young man described the affair in a letter to an overseas friend of Hermann's: "[What] a magnificent soiree Mr. Hermann gave last week, [even if the weather prevented him] from illuminating his court, and showing his fireworks....Very few failed to come—it was no doubt the finest party that had ever been given here [with] his commodious house, splendid furniture, and...good knack...."

Opposite: With its red brick facade and central entrance, this Georgian house on St. Louis Street heralded the Americanization of New Orleans. Creole features include the wrought-iron balcony railing and a large courtyard in back. Entrepreneur Samuel Hermann built the house in 1831.

Overleaf: A proper parlor of the period, Samuel Hermann's was lit with a Regency chandelier and crystal table lamps (originally with candles); the room is arranged for conversation and reading. Drapery matches the Empire chairs, covered in silk damask. Baseboards throughout the house are marbleized.

Even without the parties Hermann's house made news in New Orleans, where nothing quite like it had been seen before. Like many successful immigrants Hermann reveled in being in America, and he showed that pride even in his residence. To achieve this he hired architect-builder William Brand to create in the distinctly French and Spanish city a house that would be at home in Baltimore or Philadelphia. Not one to discard the wisdom that had shaped the Creole dwellings before him, Brand kept some European amenities in his plans, including that courtyard—one of the largest in the city. But mostly the place meant to be Yankee. While the majority of houses in the city sat at ground level, Hermann's perched a few steps from the street, with an elegant elevated entrance. Also startling was the absence of the first-level offices found in most of the old Creole places—Hermann's was extravagantly given over to living space, and that was something new and American in New Orleans. The arresting facade is Georgian, the classical style created in England during the reigns of three King Georges, from 1714 to 1820. Along the Atlantic seaboard—in the kings' former

Samuel Hermann, famous for his fortune and the way he shared it, sat for Jean J. Vaudechamp, a French portraitist who visited New Orleans in the 1830s.

American colonies—the Georgian style dominated architecture until late in the nineteenth century. The Georgian style derived its imagery and precise proportions from classical Greek and Roman forms, and on Hermann's house Ionic columns stand out in an elaborate molding that frames the arched doorway. It is a decidedly formal entrance, unlike the humble carriageway that leads to the rear of a Creole house. And where Creoles would have tall French doors, here are two exact pairs of framed windows flanking that imposing entrance. The commanding doorway and lieutenant windows are repeated on the second story, where Brand added a wrought-iron balcony, a soft touch. Without that skirt of iron, the well-ordered facade of Hermann's mansion might seem too formulaic and, in the company of its easygoing Latin neighbors, a bit pretentious. Brand originally considered Philadelphia brick, deep red and durable, but he instead used local brick to a trompe l'oeil effect, fashionable at the time. Brand painted the brick facade, then penciled the mortar, dramatically outlining each brick in white.

Inside Brand arranged things in a mostly American way, with a large central hallway running the depth of the house to a winding stair. The idea of an entrance hall providing access to various rooms was new to the old Creoles whose European custom was to step into rooms that opened onto one another. Visiting English architect Benjamin Latrobe had this to say about the two kinds of floor plans: "The English…desire that every room be separately accessible, and we consider rooms that are thoroughfares as useless. The French…employ the room they have to more advantage because they do not require so much space for passage." Nevertheless Latrobe predicted that "the American style will ultimately be that of the whole city," and he was correct. Thousands were moving to New Orleans every year, and among the newcomers were architects and carpenters trained in the English-American design that would eventually eclipse the Creole. Hermann was one of the first to try the new plan, though over the next two decades the majority of builders would follow his lead.

Hermann's first home in Louisiana was not in New Orleans but north of town, on the Mississippi River's German Coast, a community (near Baton Rouge) that Hermann's countrymen had settled a few generations earlier. Hermann probably peddled at first, later opening a dry goods store in the area. He must have felt at home among his people, for in no time he was a family man. In April of 1806, less than a year after his arrival, he married the widow Emeronthe Brou, a Catholic whose French-German ancestors had come to Louisiana in the 1720s. From her first marriage Emeronthe brought two sons, Florestan and Valsin, and she and Samuel had two boys of their own, Samuel, Jr. and Louis Florian. Hermann expanded his line of work into an array of commission sales—including slave trading—and his business ties with New Orleans were extensive. We do not know exactly when the Hermanns moved downriver, but by 1816 Emeronthe and Samuel had two more children, both born in New Orleans: Lucien and Marie-Virginie. With six children a large house must have seemed in order, and in 1823 the family moved into 820 St. Louis Street; little is known about the house except that Hermann demolished it in 1831 to make way for his Georgian mansion.

In the 1830s New Orleans entered its heyday as a major world port, a city in league with New York, Philadelphia, London. Hermann hit his stride then, too, in lucrative partnerships with other merchants and traders, and he ventured into steamboat and clipper shipping with operations up and down the Mississippi, throughout the Caribbean, and from Liverpool to New York. His chief interest, however, was as a private banker—financing loans, mortgages, stock, and real estate

sales. Hermann was only one who struck it rich in the thirties, a decade marked by wild financial speculation as the country expanded westward. Rapidly growing states were chartering banks left and right (none more than Louisiana), and these overnight (and unguaranteed) institutions extended credit quite carelessly. Competing with the banks as a moneylender, Hermann was not reckless in his credit dealings, but he was bound up with financial concerns statewide and in New York. If some faraway customers failed to pay back their loans, or if some fellow bankers seemed to be overextending credit, it did not seem to worry Samuel Hermann. As the song goes, "Who cares about a bank that fails in Yonkers?" He was having a grand time. The showplace on St. Louis Street had roundly announced the family's arrival in New Orleans society, and they were highly visible, with their parties, weddings at St. Louis Cathedral, and contributions to charities and relief funds.

Felix Grima, a Creole, bought Hermann's house in 1844; a year later he commissioned this portrait by Jacques Amans, a Belgian artist who kept a New Orleans studio.

Hermann involved his boys in his enterprises—he even named one of his ships the *Florian* after his second son.

It appears that Hermann drew no lines beween work and pleasure and entertained business associates at home. Some of his guests, like their host, were Jewish. (Among Hermann's friends was Edward Gottschalk, whose son, Louis Moreau, would become a world-famous composer.) People of many religions assimilated easily into the very Catholic city, quite free to pursue the American dream. Everything about Hermann's house announced the realization of that dream—the enormous scale of the rooms, the ornate detail in woodwork and plaster, the chandeliers and silk damask curtains. There were fine furnishings from Paris, London, New York—and New Orleans itself. Though large, the rooms in the house did not

Opposite: Corinthian columns and a carved frieze separate the parlor and dining room, where a mirror reflects candlelight. The cypress doors are faux bois—*"grained" to resemble mahogany and maple; though Samuel Hermann could have afforded the genuine article, trompe l'oeil was the fashion.*

Overleaf: The final dessert course, concluding a formal supper in old New Orleans, is set out on the Sheraton dining table. The service is a colorful Minton china, and there is crystal for sherry, port, and Madeira. The gondola chairs are attributed to the French-born cabinetmaker François Seignouret.

discourage intimacy: sliding doors between the dining room and parlor closed off either for smaller gatherings, even courtships.

Marie-Virginie was apparently a catch and had frustrated at least one suitor, a young Carl Kohn. The fellow's tactic was to suggest to Marie-Virginie that she join him in a duet at the Hermanns' parlor piano. Marie-Virginie agreed to a future date, but so reluctantly that the miffed Kohn confided in a letter to his uncle that "Miss Hermann [has] behaved most unaccountably cold to me.... I am now convinced that I could never have given her any serious cause for treating me with such marked coldness, and if it be some trifle or other, it does little credit to Miss Hermann to harbour it so long....Were that she a man I would long have asked for an explanation but with a Lady it is a delicate business." Kohn had not lost hope for the match, though, adding, "I may however yet question her about it, should I have an opportunity to play that duo with her." He was wasting his time, for Marie-Virginie married a

Offered at a réveillon, *a midnight feast on Christmas and New Year's eves, were the tall "lighthouse" cake,* croquembouche *(a pyramid of cream puffs), and other desserts of dramatic shape and presentation.*

doctor, Joseph Ursin Landreaux, in 1835. The house was ideal for such an occasion, with guests arriving in the great hallway, spilling into the rooms and through the Creole loggia onto the courtyard. And the Creole kitchen, just off the courtyard, could handle hundreds of guests.

Samuel and Emeronthe Hermann obviously preferred their traditional Creole cooking, for instead of a new American iron range, their kitchen had an open hearth, a brick oven, and a "potager." Potagers, small charcoal burners set into tile counters (also called "stew holes"), were the forerunners of stove-top cooking ranges and greatly increased the capacity of a kitchen: Hermann's cooks could braise, fry, and boil a variety of foods on the potager. Brick ovens were expensive to build and bulky; nevertheless, rich men built them to assure a good supply of home-baked breads and cakes. (New Orleans' commercial bakers were notorious for stretching flour with lime powder and cornmeal.) The cooks began their work in the cool of the morning, refiring the oven still warm from any slow overnight baking.

The kitchen staff numbered among the Hermanns' sixteen slaves, and, as director of the household, Emeronthe oversaw their work: from the rear gallery she supervised the cooking, cleaning, and gardening and also received traders, who hauled their goods into the courtyard and called prices up to her. While Emeronthe chose the gallery primarily for its strategic position over the busy courtyard and kitchen, she no doubt enjoyed its immediacy to the garden. The fragrance of the garden was not simply pleasant to the family but, so they thought, essential to health: the belief at the time was that a mingling of garden smells repelled airborne dis-

Creoles were passionate about the opera—young men sometimes dueled those who failed to share their enthusiasm for particular singers. Aristocratic families, as in this engraving, owned boxes at the French Opera House.

eases. Accordingly it became the necessary fashion to design a courtyard with one or two specimens of many different kinds of plants. In slightly raised geometric beds called parterres, the Hermanns planted native Louisiana ferns, irises, and wild strawberries; fruit trees such as lemon, orange, kumquat, and the exotic Japanese plum; heavily scented magnolias, cape jasmines, and lilies. There were also palms, bananas, and other tropical trees. The working part of the garden, near the kitchen, was the likely spot for herbs and spices—parsley, rosemary, bay, mint, pepper. (Vegetables did not grow in the garden; with fresh produce a few blocks away at the French Market, the Hermanns did not need to grow their own.) The courtyard, as richly appointed in its way as the inside of the house, was central to the Hermanns' quiet day-to-day life and to their nighttime galas.

Hermann's American dream had a long run, but it was not to last out the decade. In 1837, when banks in New York and other cities suddenly tightened credit restrictions, their peers began calling in loans, and depositors everywhere ran to get their money out of the banks. It was financial chaos, and those who had overplayed with credit faced ruin. The "Panic of 1837" hit particularly hard in New Orleans, for in addition to the national credit catastrophe, the state of Louisiana was seriously

---

Overleaf: Bedrooms of the time also served as sitting rooms, where ladies could receive friends. Madame Grima would have done so in this upstairs bedroom, furnished with upholstered rococo pieces (including the chaise longue), hand carved of mahogany in the 1850s. The fabric is brocatelle.

in debt. The city's economy would stabilize again in 1842, but Hermann's was one of many fortunes to permanently rupture. He was able to get by for a few years, first by selling off some of his most valuable possessions, then by auctioning off real estate. Hermann tried to hold on to the house, selling it to Emeronthe for a fraction of its value, but he could not even afford the maintenance. In 1844 notary Felix Grima bought the house, and his distinguished Creole family kept it for five generations. The house, now restored, is known by the names of its two owners, Hermann-Grima. Samuel Hermann never recovered financially, and both he and Emeronthe died in their daughter's care—Emeronthe in 1851, Samuel in 1853.

Hanging in the dining room of the Hermann-Grima house are separate portraits of Emeronthe and Samuel Hermann. In hers Emeronthe seems steely; look closely, though, and see her sad eyes. Samuel, to her right, is a curly haired charmer—his eyes are bright, and he is about to smile, even at his ragged ending. He looks like a man who never did expect to take anything with him.

Three 1840 vases of opaline blue glass with ormolu bases are set upon the richly worked dressing table in the upstairs bedroom. Reflected in the mirror is the globed gasolier, orginally installed for Samuel Hermann. The trompe l'oeil wallpaper, imitating the window drapery, is in the faux *fashion.*

FROM CURVES TO CURLS

New Orleans furniture at first tended toward the simple—cypress, pine, or cherry pieces without ornamentation, but with subtle curves that echoed the French Provincial style and heralded an exuberance to come. By the 1850s the vibrant city was ready for a style of furnishings that would capture the spirit of its sudden success. "The utmost luxury of decoration" is how one writer of the day described the furniture of the Rococo Revival, which was the height of fashion then in America, and nowhere more than in New Orleans. The bold curves and ornament of the Rococo Revival were inspired by earlier French designs, and in this city, the South's Gallic bastion, furniture that recalled the glories of the kings of Versailles was avidly embraced. Furniture makers produced parlor and bedroom pieces with richly carved decoration—roses and bunches of grapes were especially popular—enhanced by sumptuous upholstery. Merchants popularized the idea of matching sets of furniture, previously an almost unheard-of extravagance; these clusters of sofas, chairs, and tables made a striking impression—a profuse display of luxury. The most prominent artisans of the day were represented in New Orleans' interiors, among them New York cabinetmakers John Henry Belter and Joseph Meeks & Sons. Working in New Orleans were Frenchmen Prudent Mallard and François Seignouret, whose creations were in demand throughout the South and along the Eastern seaboard. Their armoires and beds, so finely carved and inlaid, were monumental in scale—delicate giants that perfectly suited the ample rooms of New Orleans' great houses.

A Louisiana cabinetmaker probably fashioned this armoire in the eighteenth or early nineteenth century. The armoire is large—nearly seven feet high and five feet wide—and its cabriole legs and curved panels in the Louis XV style anticipate much richer flourishes to come. The piece is made of mahogany and Spanish cedar.

*The méridienne is a small couch designed for reclining, especially for ladies in hoopskirts. This example, of lam-
inated rosewood and pale silk damask, is from Gallier House, as is the chair at right. The scrolling frame, with
its elaborate floral crest, is sculpted in the rich rococo style.*

The perforated back of this laminated rosewood chair makes a delicate counterpoint to the solid, gently curved legs and heavy velvet upholstery. The C and S curves are rococo staples. The chair, from the mid-nineteenth century, has been attributed to John Henry Belter of New York.

From its cabriole legs to the openwork crests on its high, wavy back, this sofa is of a kind de rigueur in Victorian parlors. This one, part of a parlor set made by John Henry Belter, is in 1850 House. For all its delicacy of appearance, Belter's furniture, made of multiple steam-pressed layers of laminated rosewood, is strong: it would bounce, it was said, if dropped onto a cobblestone street.

This marble-topped washstand, of rosewood with lemonwood inlay, is part of a bedroom suite by Prudent Mallard (two of its mates are opposite and on the following pages). The set is now in 1850 House.

Two cosmetic cases flank the mirror of Mallard's duchesse, *a dressing table. The light lemonwood inlay follows the luxurious lines of the piece, from the cabriole legs to the scrolled mirror frame.*

Mallard achieved dramatic effects with the inlay on the bedroom suite: the lemonwood, being almost blond, contrasts with the deep rosewood but also matches its lighter grain. In this detail of the bed's footboard, the lemonwood highlights the detailing of the rosewood frame and forms a scrolled cartouche.

3
1850 HOUSE

ROCOCO ROW HOUSE

Taken by itself, 1850 House—named for the year of its construction—could be the archetypal town house. It is much deeper than it is broad, it stands a few steps off a busy city street, and its red brick facade is precise, stately. But this house does not stand alone. It is one of sixteen in a block-long row of houses, a single building that is hard to pin down architecturally: Greek pediments crown it, rigidly proportioned doors and windows recall the Federal style, there is enough iron ornament for a few Mediterranean villas. The hybrid works somehow, the assorted details fusing into one elegant unity. Actually the final result is a double unity, for the massive row is one of two, facing its twin across Jackson Square, in the heart of old New Orleans.

Eighteen-fifty House was home to several wealthy Creole families, none of whom we know by name; plantation owners might have taken the house as their in-town residence, or new arrivals perhaps lived there while their mansions went up elsewhere in the French Quarter. To attract well-to-do residents the house had to match the best in the city, and it did. You enter 1850 House as you do most Creole houses, by following an exterior side passage—to some it seems like an alley, to others a

A freely scrolled A *and* P, *in a detail of the cast-iron balcony railings opposite, hint at the Victorian exuberance within 1850 House. The initials are for Almonester and Pontalba.*

The row houses on Jackson Square—called the Pontalba buildings, after the woman who built them— incorporate the designs of two of New Orleans' most prominent architects, Henry Howard and James Gallier, Sr. Eighteen-fifty House is in the "Lower" Pontalba, on the downriver side of the square.

Demure in this miniature on ivory, the baroness de Pontalba could be fiery when crossed. Here she wears a diaphanous gown with fashionably puffy sleeves.

variation on a porte cochere—to a rear staircase. The stairs curve above the ground-level business floor to the living quarters. Even for its relatively narrow dimension, the house rambles—up and down the wide, winding stair; between the kitchen, study, and servants' quarters off the courtyard out back; and, especially, from parlor to dining room, bedroom to bedroom. The parlor and dining room are large and high ceilinged, easily accommodating their equally large, and showy, furnishings. The third-floor bedrooms are cozier, though not to the point of crowding their suites of furniture. Fashionable New Orleanians in the mid-nineteenth century followed the more-is-more dictate of the Victorian period, and 1850 House displays those decorative essentials—theatrical layered drapery, flowered rugs over flowered carpets, porcelain vases on pedestals, portrait galleries, mirrors above marble fireplaces. Porcelain and silver collections sit for all to see on tiered rosewood sideboards.

The grandness of the house was the specific design of the rows' builder, Baroness Micaela Almonester de Pontalba. In her enthusiasm for New Orleans, she was very much like her father, Don Andrés Almonester y Roxas, a Spaniard who came to Louisiana late in the eighteenth century and built an empire in real estate. Among his prize properties were rows of shops and houses along the Place d'Armes (Plaza de Armas to the Spanish), the military parade ground laid out by the French in 1721, later renamed Jackson Square. Almonester emerged as New Orleans' greatest benefactor, and his gifts to the city include St. Louis Cathedral, the Cabildo statehouse, and the Church's presbytère (a twin of the Cabildo). Almonester died in his late seventies, leaving what was probably Louisiana's largest fortune to his only

Opposite: The hallway is a reception room, with rococo sofa and side chair (upholstered in red damask) and a mirrored hat rack; callers could compose themselves here. The sidehall is reached from the porte cochere (and offices) below: in 1850 House the Creole plan is carried out on three levels.

Overleaf: Light from the guillotine windows brightens the parlor, decorated with the Victorian passion for plenty. The rosewood pieces are all in the Rococo Revival style, some by John Henry Belter and Joseph Meeks of New York. This is also a music room: behind the harp is a rosewood baby grand piano.

surviving child. She would complete the architectural ensemble on the square with her Pontalba Rows, but that would happen many years later—after she had become the talk of two continents.

Micaela Almonester was no beauty, but she was very rich—it is not surprising that every bachelor in New Orleans pursued her, nor that she spurned them all. Her marriage, at age sixteen, was arranged in the European tradition: she did not lay eyes on her fiancé until 1811 when he arrived from France for the wedding. Celestin de Pontalba was the handsome son of a baron who had done well in France and Louisiana, though not nearly so well as Almonester. (Wags said at the time that while the bride was richer than the groom, he was prettier.) After marrying in the cathedral that Almonester had built, the newlyweds sailed off to the Pontalba château in France—and to a long and perfectly horrible life together. Micaela seemed to resent the match from the beginning, and the quiet country life was wasted on her; she was accustomed to a city pace, and she made off to Paris at every chance. With her wealth and wit, she became one of the city's renowned hostesses.

The couple filed divorce petitions back and forth, Celestin charging her with neglect, Micaela accusing all the Pontalbas of scheming after her inheritance. These were not routine in-law troubles, however. Celestin's father, the baron Pontalba, was not stable, and his clash with Micaela came to scandalous blows one night in 1834 when he failed in an attempt to murder her and then took his own life. (The drama is clouded with legendary aspects by now, but Micaela's survival of close-range gunshots evidences her indomitable constitution.) With the old man's death, his son Celestin became the baron de Pontalba and Micaela the baroness—a title she kept after the miserable marriage at last ended in 1838.

Micaela was not one to play the bitter (and literally wounded) heiress, and she eventually returned to her hometown with ambitious plans. Her timing was perfect, for Micaela's beloved neighborhood around the square, and her inherited properties that lined it, badly needed a boost. Since the late 1830s Americans had been taking over the city, moving its social and financial life to their uptown neighborhoods. New Orleans did not even sound as French as it once had, with English fast becoming the dominant language. A local writer lamented the French Quarter's fall from glory in an essay published in November 1848: "There one beholds the time-worn buildings of the old Spanish architects of the last century, crumbling and mouldering slowly away," he wrote of Andrés Almonester's house. "Even the old Place d'Armes itself has a queer, ancient, foreign look. The tall and aged sycamores

...seem to mourn as the wind whistles through them at the desolation which has crept into the old square....Where are those gay promenades, full of life and hope?"

Micaela's development scheme became a mission of urban renewal, and the zeal she brought to the project startled the town. At dealing with bureaucratic red tape, the baroness was a master: she got the city to clear the dilapidated sites, obtained an array of building permits, and even negotiated the unheard-of concession of a twenty-year tax exemption on the new construction. Micaela had arrived with definite ideas about how the buildings should look. (New Orleans historians have suggested that the baroness found her major inspiration in the Palais Royal in Paris, and the palace's arcaded wings facing each

This drapery arrangement of velvet and scalloped lace mirrors the fashions of the 1850s. The tall parlor windows rising into the ceiling give access to the gallery and its view of Jackson Square.

other across an elegant public garden do come to mind in the presence of the twin Pontalba Rows on Jackson Square.) To realize her vision she enlisted the two finest architects in New Orleans, James Gallier, Sr. and Henry Howard, though this does not necessarily reflect a philosophy of hiring the best whatever the cost: the baroness hired the best and then haggled. Gallier in fact walked off the job when Micaela balked at his fee. However little she paid for them, she got sketches and specifications from Howard, then rounded up all the contractors, laborers, and craftsmen to do the job. She broke ground in 1849, and she was there when building materials arrived: bricks from Baltimore, granite and marble from quarries in Massachusetts, cast iron from foundries in New York City. About this time New Orleans suffered another terrible plague of yellow fever, and the baroness—having had one close brush with death—took a house on the gulf coast. From that presumably safer environment, she commuted to work and was on

Overleaf: The dining room awaits midday dinner, with the soup course set on the rosewood table. The Old Paris porcelain bears the shop mark of Prudent Mallard. The mirrored sideboard, an English import, is similar in spirit to its marble-topped companion on the right, an 1850s New Orleans piece.

the job like a hard-hat supervisor: one of her contractors complained that "she put on pantaloons to go up the ladders to examine the work herself."

The houses were ready for occupancy a year later and fit for a baroness: Micaela herself took #5, and she showed its lavish rooms to prospective tenants. At the opening a daily newspaper noted that the houses in the Pontalba Rows were "elegant and convenient, inferior to none in the city. The proximity of the church and all the markets, the view of the river, the pleasant verandas which adorn the front of the buildings, and the commodious distribution of the rooms, render them particularly desirable for families...." A few months later the same newspaper urged its readers to "take their Sunday walk" in the direction of the Pontalba Rows, "to see the great improvement which our city has undergone." If all the good press were not sufficient to properly launch the Pontalba Rows, Micaela also had the good luck of a celebrity guest. Early in 1851 the singer Jenny Lind arrived in New Orleans with her impresario, P.T. Barnum, and the baroness smartly decided to prepare quarters for the "Swedish Nightingale," as Barnum billed Lind. The star loved her accommodations, said so publicly, and the remaining houses were snapped up—by the kinds of families Micaela sought. She was just as choosy about her ground-floor commercial tenants, refusing fruit vendors and coffeehouse owners for lawyers, florists, doctors, hardware dealers, jewelers. Certainly the rents the baroness charged—up to three hundred dollars monthly, an enormous sum in that day—appealed strictly to the well heeled, and 1850 House suggests the easy and very stylish living of its privileged occupants.

Luxury is obvious in the bedrooms, with their monumental Louisiana tester beds and armoires. Requisite to proper Victorian decoration were the new rococo furnishings being made in New York and New Orleans, and they are also conspicuous in 1850 House. Most notably there is a suite by John Henry Belter, a New York cabinetmaker who developed a steam process to laminate and bend rosewood. (Belter's furniture was among the most expensive of its day.) Pontalba residents could order Belter furniture from local dealers, though if pressed they would travel to New York showrooms to get it. They wanted the furniture not just because it was de rigueur but also for its practical sturdiness: Belter's tables and chairs may look as dainty as any rococo creations, but their multiple, steam-pressed layers of rosewood give them surprising weight and strength. However tough they are, the pair of Belter sofas in the parlor of 1850 House look like two frilly valentines, and the partner chairs, with their high, curly backs, are perfect accompaniment to the room's many ornate things—including a piano and harp, valued as much for their sculptural shapes as their sounds. Two rococo sideboards attend the dining table, a Louisiana treasure that seems to take up the entire room. Surrounded by upholstered chairs and set with Old Paris porcelain, the dining table recalls holiday dinners and all-day family gatherings—generously populated in the expansive Creole way. As an extension of the parlor (the two rooms are separated by massive sliding doors that today remain open), the dining room is the liveliest in the house, with the descent of raucous guests seeming imminent.

To escape the party simply step through the "guillotine" windows—named for their height—onto the front gallery. (A six-footer can get through without stooping.) Though the gallery served a practical function when servants operated pulleys to hoist up groceries, furniture, and other deliveries, its preferred role was as the family's retreat. From their iron-trimmed perch they took in the Mississippi River traffic, St. Louis Cathedral, the other Pontalba Row—and a beautiful public square.

After the opening fanfare it quickly became obvious that the Pontalba

The Pontalba Rows face each other across Jackson Square, newly landscaped as a French garden in this late-1850s view. The houses completed the architectural ensemble on the square (begun with St. Louis Cathedral)—and revitalized the Vieux Carré.

buildings had sparked a revival of commerce and glamor in the Quarter. One thing remained for Baroness Pontalba, and that was to redesign the overgrown Place d'Armes. Micaela's idea was to clear out those sad old sycamores and plant a formal French garden, with parterre beds, walkways, and rows of sculpted hedges and trees all in geometric precision. At the center of the square would be a monument to its new namesake, Andrew Jackson, hero of the Battle of New Orleans. With Jackson Square underway, the baroness returned to France. Like her father Micaela lived long—she died in Paris in 1874, at the age of seventy-nine.

Eighteen-fifty House (administered by the Louisiana State Museum) and the private houses in both Pontalba buildings still look out on the nineteenth and even eighteenth centuries. Certainly the panorama has changed—the trees in the square have grown so that they obliterate the order of the garden, there are cars, too many tourist concessions. But boats still send up whistles on the Mississippi, the river breezes blow, coffee and chicory roast at the French Market. The cathedral bells

gong on the quarter hour. In bronze Andrew Jackson waves his hat from a rearing horse. And late into the night, crowds of people buy and sell, listen to music, eat and drink. Micaela Almonester de Pontalba would approve of the street life. More than the spirit of the baroness remains along the Pontalba Rows, for her monogram—an elaborately entwined AP—was cast throughout the iron railings. It is fitting that the names Almonester and Pontalba are immortalized here, in the city that father and daughter did so much to build.

Opposite: This magnificent bed, carved of rosewood with lemonwood inlay, is from Mallard's workshop. With a mosquitaire *dropped from the tester, the bed seems almost light. Also in the suite are matching armoires, and a marble-topped nightstand, washstand, and* duchesse *dressing table.*

Overleaf: Between the mirrored armoire and the Mallard bed is a "swan" crib—the bird holds mosquito netting over the bed. A Louisiana craftsman made the rosewood crib in the late 1850s. The period portrait is of Angelle Caroline Labatut Puig, the original owner of the lemonwood-inlaid suite.

SERVICE FOR GENERATIONS

In this city known for extravagant hospitality, porcelain has held a special place among household treasures. Sunday dinners for crowds of relatives and friends were not unusual in New Orleans, and guests might stay for days. (Local lore tells of one weekend visitor who remained for twenty-seven years.) Whatever the occasion Creole and Southern delicacies and coffee were offered in abundance, and beautifully. There was fine porcelain from France, England, Germany, and Italy. The favorite seemed to be the porcelain produced in small factories that started operating in and around Paris in the late eighteenth century. Known by collectors as Vieux Paris, meaning "Old Paris," this porcelain was at first overshadowed by that of Sèvres. In the nineteenth century changing tastes and new production techniques gave Old Paris pieces a multitude of exquisite, even outlandish, shapes. Chemists achieved an astonishing range of colors, from bold chrome-greens and brick-reds to the most delicate pinks and mauves. Once a piece acquired a ground color, it was usually painted with some decoration—cornflowers were popular, as were scenes of children playing and tiny medallion portraits. Old Paris and other imported porcelain was appealing not only for its brightness and charm but also for its wonderful utility: there were serving trays, platters, and tureens, custard cups and pierced fruit baskets, pots for cream and chocolate—dozens of different pieces suitable for feasts.

Most Creoles would begin the day with café au lait—an individual service included a cup, sugar bowl, and two pitchers (one for coffee and one for hot milk). The Frankenthal porcelain factory, one of the most distinguished in eighteenth-century Germany, produced this blue-and-gold service between 1761 and 1775.

This Frankenthal tray, part of the café au lait service on page 89, is painted with a romantic scene: cupids tending to a dazed nude. (According to mythology she could be Psyche or Venus.) Entwined gold serpents form the tray's handles.

A rosy-cheeked Napoleon Bonaparte has laid down his sword in this piece of English Staffordshire, now in Pitot House. Many Creoles were Bonapartists—one group tried to arrange for the Frenchman's exile in the Vieux Carré.

A bedside veilleuse, *a small pitcher over a candlestand, was a drink warmer and a night-light. (The French name derives from* veiller, *"to keep vigil.") This one, manufactured in the 1830s, is in Hermann-Grima House.*

Arranged on a footed tray, eight small covered pots surround a ninth one raised on a pedestal in this gold-on-white service of pots de crème. Though they held sauce for entrées, pots de crème *more often appeared at dessert, filled with creams and custards. A Paris workshop produced this set in about 1820 for Bernard Colomb, a plantation owner who kept a house in New Orleans.*

A floral medallion is set against a bold pink ground on this dessert cooler. (Such pieces have an inner bowl around which crushed ice can be packed.) Pink was a particularly difficult color to achieve on porcelain; alternating with it are bands of gold and white. In the detail opposite is a tiny sculpted head, a Greco-Roman motif typical of the Empire style during the first third of the nineteenth century.

An Oriental princess and prince are portrayed in individual liqueur decanters, made about 1835 and now in Hermann-Grima House. The molds for the decanters are attributed to Jacob Petit, a Parisian artisan renowned for his painted porcelain figurines.

4
GALLIER HOUSE

VICTORIAN BY DESIGN

Much is at stake when architects design their own houses. Though we may admire their work for others, we look with more fascination at what architects scheme for themselves, when they have no clients to please. Such houses seem to reveal the architects' truest aesthetics and abilities, and anything less than perfection wounds a reputation. If James Gallier, Jr., one of the major nineteenth-century architects of New Orleans, felt those pressures when he broke ground in 1857 for his own house in the French Quarter, he was far from undone by them. The house he built on Royal Street was Gallier's best advertisement, showing the carriage trade what he could do. This house, however, was no sterile showcase unsuited to real living. On the contrary Gallier had his family very much in mind when he designed it—the neatly drawn plans were a gift to his wife, Aglae. The Galliers' four children—all daughters—shared rooms of their own, and to see the dolls and toys scattered about, it is easy to imagine that the girls had the run of the whole place. Obviously Gallier was not the sort who saved his professional skills for customers; here is a case of the cobbler's children being very well shod indeed.

Beyond a stately Italianate exterior, the Gallier house gives way inside to Victorian exuberance while also displaying up-to-date amenities. Heeding the fashions the Galliers crowded the house with the latest Rococo Revival creations, including those of New Orleans cabinetmaker Prudent Mallard. There are rosewood chairs by New York's premier rococo artisan John Henry Belter, marble-topped tables of

A cast-iron gallery, painted Paris green, a popular color in New Orleans in the mid-nineteenth century, fits over Gallier House like a Creole mask. In 1857 James Gallier, Jr. designed the town house in an Italianate style. The stucco facade is stippled and scored to resemble blocks of granite.

walnut, graceful mahogany rocking chairs, small shell-shaped sofas, hand-carved sideboards, elaborate plant stands, and gold-framed mirrors. Baseboards are painted to imitate the black marble framing each fireplace, and high-relief plaster moldings along the ceilings seem lifted from a Louis XV rococo palace. Dense patterns of flowers and vines crawl over carpets, wallpapers, even window shades. Curtains and cornices would suit the grand opera. For all the opulence and the sheer volume of things, though, this is not a fussy house: these flowery rooms with their curvaceous chairs are dignified and inviting.

Part of this comfort comes from Gallier's elaborations on the basic sidehall town house, which made the plan more responsive to the individual needs of his family. A sidehall is just that—a hallway that runs along one side of a house—and Gallier's opens onto a grand double parlor, the twin rooms separated by square columns, their Corinthian capitals brightly gilded. In the nineteenth century double parlors logically developed in New Orleans and other cities where narrow lots restricted what an architect could do. Running deep rather than wide, double parlors paired rooms that would be across a hall from each other in houses of greater breadth. Sliding doors divided some double parlors, though a screen of imposing columns such as Gallier's was often sufficient to break a ballroom-size space. The rooms are ready for a variety of activities: there are quiet corners for reading, game tables, a writing desk, a piano, groupings of seats for conversation. Past the parlors are an elegant dining room, served by a spacious pantry, and a kitchen equipped with all that was modern—such as a copper boiler (providing hot water for the entire house) and a cast-iron range fired by anthracite. Gallier laid the kitchen and bathroom floors with a material called "kamptulicon," the forerunner of linoleum. The kamptulicon here is patterned with maroon medallions on a beige background.

Back at the front hallway, a staircase ascends to Gallier's library, lined with walnut bookcases and illuminated by a skylight. The library did double duty as the second-floor hallway, opening into each of the family's upstairs rooms, which had

Opposite: Next to the parlor méridienne (a small sofa designed to accommodate a lady's ample skirts) is a papier-mâché end table, holding crochet. The fern is one of many: Victorians advocated the decorative quality and healthful benefits of plants—their parlors were veritable greenhouses.

Overleaf: Divided by square Corinthian columns, the two halves of the double parlor are united by rich details and decoration: the relief of plaster cornices and moldings, matching gasoliers (of bronzed gunmetal), the French trompe l'oeil wallpaper, and the intimate groupings of rococo furniture.

their own connecting doorways. This ingenious plan let Gallier hole up with his books (there were over a thousand volumes stacked in those tall cases) and gave Mrs. Gallier private access to her study; the girls, meanwhile, could slip in and out of their rooms without disturbing their parents. In his and Aglae's bedroom, Gallier added a built-in closet. A single bathroom served the bedrooms, but what a bathroom it was: there were faucets for hot and cold water, a newfangled water closet, a shiny copper tub set into a walnut cabinet. Beyond these private rooms are a breezy gallery and the service wing, a sunny row overlooking the courtyard. The four servants' quarters here are spare but handsomely furnished with the family's castoffs—four-poster beds, cypress armoires, comfortable upholstered chairs. Even in the storage rooms and in such details as shelving, Gallier proved himself an exacting professional.

Gallier had learned much of his craft from his father. Gallier, Sr. had joined the rush to Louisiana in the early 1830s, rightly reckoning that the dynamic city on the Mississippi would offer design competitions for new public buildings and that its new millionaires would need mansions. Strong classical references in Gallier's work reflected his passion for antiquity and his training before he immigrated to America. Though the name does not sound it, Gallier was Irish: it had been Gallagher. Little of the family's history is known, and it is tempting to say that Senior changed his name to the more Gallic-sounding Gallier in order to make it in New Orleans' French Creole society. That, though, was not the case. The change of name had occurred a generation or two before him, in Ireland. Already a Gallier, James, Sr. attended the School of Fine Arts in Dublin, then went to London to practice architecture. There he married Elizabeth Tyler, who in 1827 bore James, Jr., the couple's only child to survive infancy. The Galliers doted on the boy and, in America, sent him to fine schools in New York (where they lived for a brief time), Mississippi, and North Carolina. Together in New Orleans father and son emerged as high-society architects, building Italianate mansions, banks and houses in the Greek Revival style, and dignified French Quarter residences that, except for the inevitable flourishes of ironwork, could have been cut from rows of houses in London. As an elderly widower Senior fancied himself a citizen of the world, and he

---

The three graces of Greek mythology are posed between tassled damask drapery. The gilded mirror, positioned across the parlor from its twin, multiplies the golden illumination above the marble figures. Victorians were fond of classical statuary: in the Gallier parlor there are nine such pieces.

became just that, turning over his partnership to his son so that he (and his second wife) could travel. (In his autobiography Senior describes the sights from Italy to New York, stopping along the way to refer to the highlights of his career.) He returned to New Orleans now and then, to look in on the Gallier architectural legacy, probably making a special trip in 1853 for his son's wedding. While James's marriage to Aglae, of the distinguished Villavaso family, no doubt pleased his father, it is likely that the couple disappointed the old man by presenting him not a single grandson. Senior, though, could have no quarrel with the charmed life that James provided Aglae and the four daughters—Leonie, Josephine, Clemence, and Blanche.

Living in their splendid house, the six Galliers were at the center of the city, though they were also at a civilized remove from the hubbub. Gallier was not, after all, a get-rich-quick trader, but an architect, an artist. The house and its appointments reveal those things important to the family: there were parlor games and music, a love of painting and sculpture, and entertaining (the porcelain and silver could serve a large party, and there were 150 bottles of claret and white wines in storage). And the Galliers read. Though most of the books were in his library, Mrs. Gallier kept a few in her study, most of them dealing with domestic issues. This was the day of household manuals, etiquette books, child-rearing guides, anything on self-improvement. Easily the most popular counselor was Catherine Beecher (sister of Harriet Beecher Stowe, the famous author of *Uncle Tom's Cabin*). Catherine Beecher wrote eleven books, all of them stressing the social and economic importance of the domestic sphere. *A Treatise on Domestic Economy*, Beecher's best-seller published in 1845, became the bible of homemakers and mothers. Mrs. Gallier would refer to the book certainly not to learn about making soap or ironing a crease, but for Beecher's personal philosophy and extensive advice on household management. She would make sure, for example, that her servants had memorized each step in the section called "On Sweeping and Cleaning a Parlor." Nor could Mrs. Gallier ignore

Opposite: The parlor is dressed for summer with rush matting, simplified window treatments, and muslin slipcovers. Mosquito netting over the gasolier and mirror protects bronzed and gilded finishes from insects. The lacquered kidney-shaped table is set for a game of patience (much like solitaire).

Overleaf: The Galliers' kitchen had everything modern. A cast-iron range is built into the hearth, and the copper boiler next to it provided hot running water. The walls were whitewashed every spring to freshen the room. Fixings for gumbo, the famous Creole specialty, are spread out on the pine table.

outdoor scene developed early in the Quarter, with men and women chatting across iron railings, children hollering from gallery to gallery.

So went the lovely times on Royal Street. What paid for them were Gallier's commissions, which continued through the Civil War. (When Union troops peacefully occupied the city in 1862, business there hardly missed a beat.) Gallier even built houses for carpetbaggers who came early to New Orleans, before the war was over, and he was by no means alone in serving the Yankees. New Orleans was free in a sense—Southern, yes, part of the Confederacy, but commerce got the first salute. Among Gallier's largest jobs was one for businessman Florence Luling, who asked for a lavish Renaissance villa off of Esplanade Avenue. Gallier delivered, but apparently went overboard: Luling had to urge him in a letter to please keep down the cost. Gallier had surpassed that mansion's grandeur in his most important city commission, the French Opera House, which he designed as much for a rubbernecking audience as the art: from tier to tier operagoers had unobstructed views of one another.

The servants' rooms, in the wing over the courtyard, are furnished with essentials: this one has a high-post bed, a short Louisiana armoire, and a washstand of cypress. The hip bath is made of zinc.

This father-son story has a sudden and somewhat strange ending. The ever-voyaging Mr. and Mrs. Gallier, Sr. were apparently having a fine time in October 1866, sailing from New York to New Orleans on the *Evening Star*. They shared the elegant ship with the twenty-two members of New Orleans' French Opera, returning from a tour to the Gallier opera house. The *Evening Star*, however, never got its passengers home: the steamer went down in the

Opposite: Aglae Gallier's sitting room was also her office for household accounts and correspondence. Behind the lacquered table, set for tea, is a mirror-lidded sewing box. The Victorian preference for floral patterns is evident in the carpet, cornices, wallpaper, needlepoint, and porcelain.

Overleaf: Two of the Gallier daughters shared this bedroom, ready for a summer tea party. The smaller dolls are mid-nineteenth century; the larger one is from the 1890s. There are also a pine rocking horse and, on the pine dresser, a doll's dressing table. The pine bed is stenciled with flowers.

Atlantic and there were no survivors. Gallier, Jr. died just two years later, perhaps succumbing to yellow fever, though no exact cause was recorded. He had lived in his house barely a decade. With his untimely death (he was forty-one), New Orleans lost a premier architect in his prime, and Royal Street gradually lost its glow. The Gallier women kept the residence until 1917, after which it fell into disrepair and was virtually forgotten—it was not until the 1960s that new owners rescued the house. A private foundation was eventually established to restore the address to Gallier's standards; in 1974 Gallier House was named a national historic landmark.

On hot summer days the back gallery was an ideal spot to have guests for pink lemonade. Set on the cherry drop-leaf table are grenadine-filled glasses, crushed ice, a lemon press, and a full pitcher. The caned rocking chair is from the girls' room, which is through the silk-curtained window.

FAMILY PORTRAITS
BY A MASTER

Late in 1872 the French artist Edgar Degas left his studio in Paris to come to New Orleans. It was a family visit, for Degas had many relations in Louisiana: his mother was from a prominent Creole family, the Mussons, and two of his brothers, René and Achille, had moved from France to join the Musson cotton business. Suffering from an eye disorder, Edgar seemed not in a good temper throughout his visit, and he found the Louisiana sun too intense (even in winter). Still, he admired much about New Orleans, and his letters to friends in France are unmistakably those of an artist observing new scenes. "Everything attracts me here," begins one letter describing the Creole cottages, steamboats, French market, orange gardens, and especially the different people. "Nothing pleases me so much as the [women] of every shade," he wrote, "and the children all in white, and so snow white cradled in black arms." Setting up a studio in the Musson mansion on Esplanade Avenue, Degas began to make drawings and paintings of his uncle, brothers, cousins, nieces, and nephews—in individual sittings, together in rehearsals (the Mussons were a musical family), and at work. Degas's *The Cotton Office in New Orleans* (pages 126–127) is the best-known work from his stay. Though he finally found the Louisiana light "impossible" and returned to Paris early in 1873, Degas did produce a series of touching family portraits in New Orleans.

Two Musson sisters—Estelle on the left with either Mathilde or Désirée—rehearse an opera scene in Degas's oil on canvas. René Degas, Estelle's husband and the artist's brother, accompanies the women at the piano.

Estelle Musson, in Degas's oil painting at left, arranges flowers not by sight but by touch and fragrance: the woman had been struck blind at the age of twenty-three. The artist made vivid only Estelle's most immediate, tactile surroundings—the gladiolus, zinnias, and chrysanthemums, the vase and pitcher on the drop-leaf table, the subject herself. In contrast to this color and clarity are the broad strokes that indicate the background, the unknown world beyond Estelle's reach. With his own eyesight weakening, Degas took a special interest in Estelle—his portraits of her are the most realized of all the ones he made of his female cousins—and his observations of her were full of empathy and admiration. "My poor Estelle," he wrote, "is blind. . . . [But] she endures it in an amazing way. . . . She has mastered her misfortune."

123

Mathilde Musson sat for Degas in December, though the picture suggests summertime: the young woman wears a light dress and holds a fan. For this drawing of his youngest cousin, Degas used pencil and chalk.

This oil canvas is also known as La Malade *("The Invalid"), an appropriate title for the enervated subject, the eldest cousin of the artist. Degas favored Désirée as a model, particularly for her long hands.*

THE COTTON OFFICE IN NEW ORLEANS

The most ambitious work of Degas's time in New Orleans is the oil painting at right, of a typical workday inside the family cotton office. Michel Musson, Degas's uncle, was a cotton broker, acting between planters and their wholesale and international customers; among his partners were the artist's brothers René and Achille. The Creoles and Frenchmen went about their business at an unhurried Latin pace, and Degas painted a languid scene of his family at work: Michel Musson is in the foreground, inspecting a swatch of cotton; behind him is René, reading the Times-Picayune; *at the extreme left, leaning against the window, is Achille. Various partners of the Musson firm are on hand, showing samples from different bales of cotton and inspecting account books.*

5
STRACHAN HOUSE

CONFEDERATE DREAMS

In the two decades before the Civil War, New Orleans saw a new kind of aristocrat come to town. These late arrivals were Americans, many of them from plantations along the Mississippi River. Snubbed by the Creoles, they attempted to outdo the elegance of the Vieux Carré by building their own houses uptown across Canal Street, which became the divide between the city's American and European sectors. These lands above the old city lay in large plantations, and it was up to the Americans to develop them into residential areas that would appeal to the new breed of New Orleanian. The development could hardly miss, and, before long, fine houses—quite different from the ones downtown—began to appear along the newly cut streets. The best of the American neighborhoods was the Garden District, and in the 1850s an address there became essential to correct social standing. Jacob U. Payne was one of the privileged newcomers who decided to build a place in New Orleans. Originally from the horse country of Kentucky, Payne had gone to Louisiana, where he became a successful cotton planter; with his eventual move to New Orleans, he and his wife, Charlotte, traveled the important distance to the very center of the nation's cotton trade. Payne's house, a Greek Revival edifice on First Street, was called a showplace when it went up in 1850, and that remains a fair designation for what is now known as the Strachan house, after its owners, Mr. and Mrs. Frank G. Strachan. (Mrs. Strachan's mother, Mrs. William Bradish Forsyth, restored the house in the 1930s.)

The double portico of Strachan House, with Grecian columns and cast-iron railings, exemplifies the Greek Revival style in the Garden District: a classical plan suiting a subtropical climate. The capitals are also of cast iron, from an Eastern foundry—they are stamped "New York 1848."

Little is known about Jacob Payne, but surely he had his expansive side—the cosmopolitan Garden District, with its impressive architecture, attracted the most social of men. Payne possibly designed the house himself (bringing slaves from his plantation to build it), a not unusual task in a day when gentlemen were expected to be many things—dabblers, as Renaissance men, in art, music, architecture. Not educated as an architect, Payne would have relied on a number of popular stylebooks of the day, particularly *The Modern Builders Guide* by Minard Lafever, a New York architect. Lafever had once been in partnership with James Gallier, Sr. when the latter lived in New York in the early 1830s, and both men were champions of the Gothic and Greek revivals that were having a strong effect on the national architecture at

A pavilion rising above mounded boxwoods echoes the classical facade of the Strachan house. The tranquil gardens are planted and appointed in a way imitating formal French and Italian landscaping.

the time. (Gallier eventually moved to New Orleans and encouraged his son, James, Jr., in architecture; among the younger's renowned works is his own residence, the subject of the previous chapter) Lafever's *The Modern Builders Guide*, published in 1833, combines history with how-to—it contains basic geometry lessons, glossaries of builders' terms, descriptions of tools and procedures. There are simple drawings to suggest what is proper in the way of front entrances, window frames and shutters, sliding parlor doors, staircases and handrailings, moldings for walls and doorways. Lafever was a stickler for native and traditional building materials, and, a good classicist, he encouraged restraint in design. Payne for the most part seems to have followed Lafever's advice: the proportions of the Strachan house, and the details,

Opposite: The entrance hall—the axis of the house—is a breezeway leading straight to the gardens. The walls of Wedgwood blue set off the millwork framing the doorways and the carved ceiling frieze. The staircase is all mahogany, contrasting with the floors of pine.

Overleaf: Pale green walls, a pink silk brocade (over the 1750 English sofa), and muted colors in needlepoint pillows set a quiet mood for reading and taking tea in the Strachan library. The bookcase, also an English piece, blocks the sliding doors, which lead into the guestroom.

131

inside and out, are just right. The workmanship—in wood, plaster, and iron—is superior, and it is clear that there were fine craftsmen and artisans among Payne's unsung laborers.

Approaching the house you are initially struck by a certain might, for it is difficult to be blasé in the face of such strong Grecian columns, so finely turned, so white in the New Orleans sun. There are actually two tiers of columns—Ionic below and Corinthian above. The upper portico encloses a veranda, or, as New Orleanians have preferred to call it, a gallery. Sweet olive trees soften the looming facade and make the house approachable; getting a closer look you see that ornate cast-iron railings surround the porch and gallery. The ironwork is not remotely classical, but quintessentially Creole: apparently Payne did not entirely go by the book. This house is an indigenous hybrid, as suited to the local climate and customs as one in the Vieux Carré. The cool gallery and other casual touches throughout the place relax an otherwise rigid formula of design, and make for easy living. For all its precise proportion and detail, this home is only as formal as the elements and good sense would allow.

The face of things is so well balanced it seems that one extra louver in a shutter could throw off the whole scheme. There are a dozen columns, six up and six down. The front entrance, subtly sculptural, has a paneled door flanked by sidelights in hand-carved frames; to either side are sash windows, as tall as the doorway— shuttered against the rain and wind, they function as French doors do on the downtown houses. The arrangement of windows and doors is duplicated, shutter for shutter, on the veranda, and the exactitude can be intimidating. The impulse is to straighten your necktie before you ring the bell.

Invited in, you step into the central hallway, where servants once took coats and hats before gesturing to the right, toward the parlor. Furnished in the way that parlors are, with chairs grouped for conversation, the parlor is also an anteroom to the formal scene lying beyond a pair of sliding doors. This is the dining room, and, fitted with a custom china cabinet and lit by an eighteenth-century chandelier, it pricks the imagination: it would be a waste if many Southern banquets had not been spread out on that long mahogany table. (In old New Orleans even breakfast was a

---

The centerpiece of the rose parlor is the gilded mirror, extending to the frieze—Jacob Payne ordered the glass from Paris in 1848, and it was a fine companion to the fireplace of gold-veined marble. The round American Empire table has its own golden detail: an ormolu swan is attached to each foot.

multicourse affair to be lingered over. One breakfast menu of the time listed "Chicken a la Creole, Kidney with Tomato Sauce, Veal Omelet, Mayonaise of Fish, Stuffed Tomatoes, Pineapple with Port Wine, Coffee." The coffee was the Creole version—roasted with chicory and served with steaming milk, as café au lait.) Across the hallway is another pair of rooms, first a library, then a guestroom. There is commerce between the rooms, from front to rear and across the hallway. And opening up each are those tall windows, their drapery disturbed all day by breezes. In the parlor and library it is nothing to raise one of the windows above your head and step onto the front porch.

The stairway is not centered in the hallway but to one side of it. Its mahogany railing leads to a second floor that repeats what has gone below—four rooms, two to either side of the axis hallway. Though these are the private family quarters and so removed from scrutiny, Payne's men did not alter the standards they had set constructing the more public, social rooms downstairs: the plaster walls here are as smooth as marble, the doorframes and wall moldings are a carver's pride. In Payne's day these rooms looked over the goings-on of a very social neighborhood— St. Charles Avenue was the scene of evening promenades where groups of gents tipped their hats to ladies passing by in carriages. More privileged socializing in the Garden District was of course carried on in houses and gardens such as the Paynes'. Stepping to her bedroom window, Mrs. Payne could survey her own garden parties in order to properly time her descent.

The Strachan garden, in fact, is laid out in a way best appreciated at some elevated distance. Unlike the courtyards in the Vieux Carré, conceived as miniature jungles, uptown gardens were carefully delineated with boxwoods and other bushes trimmed and shaped just so. The Americans created architectural landscapes with little pathways leading to pavilions and gazebos, and classical sculpture placed here and there. The green is everywhere in the Strachan garden, and something is in bloom year round: there are magnolias here, and gardenias, crepe myrtles, night-blooming jasmines, camellias, oleanders. There is also Confederate rose, its flower beginning the day white, turning pink and nearly red as the sun goes down. It is easy to imagine parties in this formal yet fragrant and colorful setting, with music

---

The Empire secretary, of walnut with trompe l'oeil inlay, displays family treasures— including, at the left on the bottom shelf, a Capodimonte urn owned by Jefferson Davis, president of the Confederacy. The pilasters framing the secretary rise to the frieze, adding to the room's classical formality.

rising from a pavilion and the lawn almost white with parasols and summer jackets. Payne's guests were no doubt a happy lot, caught up in the good fortune of being in New Orleans in the 1850s, the city's answer to the best of times. This house, a veritable flagship in the Garden District, was at the center of the hubbub—and it was also part of what came after.

One incident that involved the house during the Civil War still amuses New Orleanians, though no one was laughing when it happened. Union troops took over the city in 1862 in peaceful maneuvers that nonetheless displaced many owners of New Orleans' finest houses. The Yankees needed headquarters during the occupation, and the officers among them had standards to match their ranks. General Benjamin F. Butler had his eye on a Garden District mansion, but it belonged to a British citizen who announced that he would not vacate it—wartime law did not compel him to do so. Jacob Payne had no such defense when Butler next came for his house. Forced to return to his plantation, Payne managed, before leaving the city, to bury much of the family silver under the rosebushes but had to abandon other treasures—Turkish rugs, chandeliers, porcelain, entire rooms of French furniture. Payne reclaimed his house after the war and found it in good order (including the silver, undisturbed beneath the roses). He did, however, discover a surprise in the dining room, now filled with things he had never before seen—his furniture apparently had been part of some swap between generals. It was a fine suite that Payne had unwittingly inherited, perfectly suitable for dinner parties, and he shrugged off the incident. But one night a guest broached a touchy subject: "I hate to say this," he reportedly said to his host, "but we are sitting on my chairs and eating off my table." The room fell silent but the tense moment was broken by laughter— Payne's. The claimant guest no doubt appreciated the joke, too, when Payne paid him for the furniture.

This is one of the few stories told about Jacob and Charlotte Payne. More is known about their daughter, Caroline, who married a Louisiana Supreme Court justice, Charles E. Fenner, to whom the house passed when the Paynes died in the 1870s. Jefferson Davis, the former president of the Confederacy, was a friend of the Fenners' (as he had been of the Paynes'), and he often stayed with them on First Street,

The dining room's low light is reflected in the mate of the parlor mirror. English Chippendale chairs are gathered around the mahogany table, divided by four Georgian candlesticks and set for the evening's final course. The rug adds subdued colors to the room: rose, dark blue, and blue-green.

arriving by carriage or boat from Beauvoir, his gulf coast estate near Biloxi, Mississippi. The Fenners also entertained a younger generation whose members included the children of the defeated Confederates. Davis's daughter, Varina Ann (known as Winnie), was among the guests, along with the daughters of generals Robert E. Lee, Stonewall Jackson, and D.H. Hill. The premier social event of these years was the debut of Winnie Davis, in a lavish presentation and ball at the Fenners' house. As First Street saw the rise of this new generation, and the very beginnings of a different South, it also saw the end of the Confederacy's chief elder. Jefferson Davis had not been in good health before his surrender (in 1865), and his condition was exacerbated by the Northern captors who had shackled him in a dank cell. Davis had spent the years since the war in convalescence, writing at home and traveling. New Orleans offered him not only a pleasant change of scene, but supportive company: the Fenners and their guests were probably like many Southerners who in some way still considered the charismatic statesman their leader. In December 1889 Davis fell gravely ill and died at the Fenners', in the downstairs guestroom. Davis's funeral befitted a president and perhaps provided the occasion to bury an old conflict: above the gold-handled casket United States and Confederate flags crossed, like a tense embrace.

People came to regard the house as a shrine, and on occasion a few bold ones would ring the bell, to ask Charles and Caroline Fenner, or their children, if they could see the room where Jefferson Davis had died. This house has the odd distinction of being both a historic site and a private home. The Strachan family acknowledges that status: there are certainly no tour guides on duty, but there is a stone marker out front, near the street, that reads in part: "Here in the home of his friend, Jefferson Davis, first and only president of the Confederate States of America ...died." Chiseled into the side facing the house is a poem that begins: "Take to thy heart O Southland/This thy son...."

Opposite: The black marble mantel holds porcelain suitable for a soiree; twin Empire vases flank a gold-and-white compote. The Parisian mirror, original to the house, reflects the Waterford chandelier (circa 1780) and a portrait of William Forsyth, Mrs. Strachan's great-grandfather.

Overleaf: With a tester bed of dark mahogany, the beige-and-rose guestroom is a quiet retreat, lightened by a garden view: azaleas and boxwoods appear beyond the cast-iron balcony. Jefferson Davis, a frequent overnight guest of the Payne and Fenner families, died in this room in 1889.

ALFRESCO HIDEAWAYS

In the Vieux Carré iron gates and arched passageways offer constantly recurring glimpses into a world of carefully nurtured intimate gardens: a world of privacy at once revealed and reserved. On through a passageway one emerges in a walled courtyard, filled with vines, hedges, trees, flowers—and, among all the plants, little pools and fantastic iron griffins clinging to the rims of small fountains. The most powerful impression of these hidden gardens is of green: the green of boxwood, wisteria, sweet olive, and aspidistra. Azaleas and camellias are red, pink, coral, and white, and there are the colors of oleanders, magnolias, night-blooming jasmines, lemon and orange trees, pomegranates, Japanese plums, kumquats. New Orleans is a tropical hothouse, and things grow in profusion and fill the courts with fragrances. These private retreats, originally laid out as carriageways and working areas, are like nothing so much as informal outdoor living rooms, furnished with iron furniture, cool to the touch. The ideal of the French garden is everywhere evident: the clipped hedges defining concise walkways, the trees and plants set out with such order and design. And yet the climate is such, and the vegetation, and the nature of things, that the vines and flowers growing in New Orleans' courtyards cannot be entirely civilized: they are lush, luxuriant, nearly wild.

An iron lantern marks the entrance to a secluded and shady retreat, paved with bricks and flagstones. Against the rear brick wall, a table is surrounded by delicate iron chairs and set with a pot of bright impatiens (the same flower that is planted at the iron gates). Among the trees are pear, orange, and kumquat.

Ferns grow in pots and from the cracks and crevices of a tiny courtyard's old brick wall. Wisteria—all green here but lavender in bloom—makes a sort of garland along the staircase. Nearly unnavigable for the plants, the stairs lead to the roof of the courtyard carriage house.

A calla lily sprouts from a pool in the bricked courtyard of Soniat House, built in 1830. Lilies and palmettos bank the pool, which is fed by water trickling from a dolphin into an overflowing shell basin. The courtyard, both sunny and shady, is home to various green and flowering plants—and goldfish.

Here on a grand scale are all the elements of a classic Vieux Carré courtyard: fountain, marble statuary, curly cast-iron furniture, and things growing in the ground, in pots, and in baskets. A magnolia tree shades the entire

courtyard. Dr. Joseph Montegut, a surgeon, built the house in 1795 and entertained in this courtyard—among his guests were royalist refugees from the French Revolution.

149

One of the most secretive hideaways in New Orleans, this courtyard is double chambered: the bricked half in the foreground, accessible only through a sidewalk gate, is an anteroom to its grassy counterpart beyond. In pots and raised brick beds, the courtyard hoards caladiums, water hyacinths, impatiens, and ferns.

A stone goddess stands in an arbor of white flowering vines—an elegant and not unusual scene in a quiet Vieux Carré courtyard. Imitating the great gardens of French royalty, Creoles placed classical images—of stone or iron— in even the smallest of their courtyards.

Brick walkways radiate from an octagonal pool in a tree-shaded courtyard. The beds are given over to expanses of grass.

Pink caladiums color the foreground.

6

MADDOX-BRENNAN HOUSE

ORDER AND OPULENCE

A few blocks from the Strachan house (Chapter Five) is one of the grandest Greek Revival mansions in New Orleans. In spite of its scale and classical styling, the house has something of the Creole spirit—it might be seen as the Garden District's answer to the Hermann-Grima house (Chapter Two), the Georgian-Creole blend in the Vieux Carré. This house on Prytania Street has all the beauty that derives from the perfection of classical proportions, but Creole amenities here and there give character to its pretty face. You immediately see that, like a good Creole cottage, this house has made peace with the environment—it sits under the shade of trees, and it mixes indoors and out, with wide open windows, a large gallery above a front porch, and a little balcony on one side. Originally the house had a rear wing, much like the *garçonnière* behind the Hermann-Grima house; adjacent to where the wing once stood there is still a modest courtyard—a surprise in a neighborhood famed for its noble gardens.

The builder of the house, Joseph Maddox, turns up only fleetingly in local antebellum histories, which is odd considering his prominent position: Maddox was the publisher of the New Orleans *Daily Crescent*, one of the city's seven newspapers at the time. Property records do state that in 1852 Maddox bought a "quarter square" of land at Prytania and Second streets. (That measure was relative, depending on the size of a particular city block—in this case the lot was approximately 250 by 150 feet.) To design the house Maddox commissioned local architect John Barnett, who then turned over the project to a colleague, Edward Gotthiel, to supervise every

The stately columned entrance of the Maddox-Brennan house, visible from the cast-iron gates, is recessed beneath the gallery. Local architect John Barnett designed the Prytania Street residence for a party-giving client: among the original thirty rooms is a palatial ballroom.

stage of construction. (Gotthiel's fee is on record as six hundred dollars.) The use of two architects—one to produce detailed plans for an overall scheme and another to work in a supervisory capacity—was not an uncommon professional practice of the day. It allowed the designing architect to focus on the art and theory of his profession while leaving the day-to-day details to someone else. A third party, John K. Eichelberger, worked with Barnett and Gotthiel as a contractor, rounding up the carpenters, bricklayers, plasterers, and other laborers and artisans, and acquiring the materials (ranging from local cypress to such imports as West Indian mahogany and Italian black marble). As the work progressed, Gotthiel would make minor changes, elaborating on Barnett's drawings as needed. One of the other spare facts known about Joseph Maddox is that he did not keep his house for long, losing it in bankruptcy proceedings later in the decade. The house has had several owners since Maddox's sudden misfortune, and today it goes by the names of its first and current families, Maddox-Brennan. Though the house fell into disrepair from time to time, it has been in the hands of restoration-minded owners since its centennial in the 1950s, and it appears now much as it did when Maddox, the powerful publisher, received the elite of New Orleans' business, political, and social worlds.

The Maddox-Brennan house is sequestered in a grove of oaks and palms that obscures a facade as assertive as that of the Strachan house. The Maddox-Brennan house shows through a parting in the trees: you see the white-on-white entrance, a paneled door framed by four Doric columns. To get closer you must be admitted past the spiky iron gate; the whole comes into view as you proceed down the walkway to the far side of the trees. The Greek Revival styling here is the double-tiered kind, with a portico supported by Ionic columns on the lower level and Corinthian above. There are the familiar cast-iron railings around the porch and gallery—a pattern of arabesques and arrows below, something floral and vaguely heart-shaped above. The spirited ironwork lightens the somber colonnade and seems to make a friendly

---

Opposite: The parlor appears through sliding doors, slightly parted; made of burl walnut, they frame what lies beyond. Afternoon sun lights the silk-striped walls and matching drapery and the twin Chippendale sofas. The gilded wall clock is a late-eighteenth-century piece from France.

Overleaf: Arranged for an intimate group, the golden parlor suits the individual as well: the small Chinese Chippendale table on the right is set for one. Joseph Maddox also used the room as a library, filling it with books. The windows rise to the ceiling, opening the room to the porch.

gesture: a rocking chair or two would complete this homey scene. But this front porch, so welcoming, is the last touch of informality for a while—inside there is no place for an old rocker.

The entrance hall is a considerable room of its own, running the depth of the house and appropriately appointed for waiting and receiving: here is where a caller would sit until Maddox came down from his study. The extravagant use of different woods lends a special texture to the hallway; its floor is of polished pine, and cypress, walnut, and mahogany went into the staircase. But it is the plaster cornices trimming the length and breadth of the ceiling that most distinguish the hallway. A plasterer's masterwork, the cornices are perforated in an openwork design and are set out at a slight angle—you can see through them to the juncture of wall and ceiling. Sunlight and chandelier-light play through the openwork, adding to the richness of the room. Other rooms in the house must rise to these standards.

To the right of the hallway is a parlor, its walls covered with bands of gold silk— they glow in the morning and evening sun. The room makes the porch its own extension, with the sheer curtains blowing in and out of the twelve-foot-high windows. During a rare cold snap, company would turn toward the parlor's fire-place, which is considered one of the most beautiful in the city. The mantel of burl walnut is matched by the parlor's sliding doors, which are set in a frame carved to resemble folds of drapery. Parted, these doors reveal the dining room, which, like the parlor, is a perfect square and a shade of gold. Though the dining room is an altogether formal space, with a Queen Anne table and Chippendale chairs beneath a Waterford crystal chandelier, the decorative detail around the fireplace adds a refreshing regional motif to the room as well. Framing the hearth is a series of tiles painted with a wildlife scene—herons and other native Louisiana birds nested in an eerily beautiful swamp. For a moment you might think you were in a little cabin far from the civilized streets of the Garden District. Together, parlor and dining room can be treated as a double parlor, though architect Barnett intended the latter specifically as a dining room—it has easy access to the kitchen and pantry through a discreet doorway.

In the rich years before the Civil War, Maddox and his peers ate and drank in elegant, and correct, settings. Even soirees, more casual than dinner parties, were brought off according to precise rules of etiquette. For "evening parties" a domestic manual of Maddox's day issued specific instructions: "Cover...a long table in the dining room...with a handsome damask cloth. Set some high article containing flowers, or some ornamental article, in the center....Where a very large company is to be collected, and a larger treat is thought to be required...then smaller tables are set each side of a mantel, or in corners....A great deal of taste may be displayed in preparing and arranging [tables]." Maddox's dining table could seat twenty-five (it is listed in the household inventory as a "magnificent extension table of carved oak"), and the late evening fare would include shrimp and oyster hors d'oeuvres, delicate chicken sandwiches, and an array of fruitcakes, sugar-coated pecans, ladyfingers, and petits fours. And there would be port, sherry, champagne, Madeira, liqueurs, and coffee.

New Orleans society turned out in 1879—as they had before and have since—for the Grand Ball of Rex, the culminating celebration of the Mardi Gras season. In this engraving the gentlemen wear white tie and tails, and the ladies eye one another's gowns.

In the Maddox-Brennan house the evening included dancing. Across the hallway is a ballroom so opulent it made the house famous when it was built, and people are still curious to see it. In a city with lavish public facilities, few bothered to build their own ballrooms; that Joseph Maddox did so, and in such a big way, indicates the man's social bent. The ballroom is nearly fifty feet long, with gold and silver mirrors reflecting the impressive fixtures and details: there are twin Baccarat chandeliers, two marble fireplaces, windows draped as if they were small proscenium stages. There is so much gilt along the walls and ceiling that this is known as the Gold Room. An archway, aloft on gilded Corinthian columns, divides the room so that it recalls a fancy double parlor, such as the one in Gallier House (Chapter Four). Though this can be used as a double parlor (and has been referred to as such), it was probably conceived as a ballroom: the oak floor seems designed for dancers, with its boards laid diagonally for dramatic effect, and there is a small adjacent room for musicians. This ballroom would become one of New Orleans' more spectacular private settings for wedding receptions, debutante parties, and the many balls that filled the local calendar — including those during Mardi Gras.

Overleaf: Golden like the parlor it adjoins, the dining room also has tall windows that open onto a porch defined by cast iron. On pleasant evenings guests could socialize on the porch while waiting to be seated for supper at the mahogany extension table. The chairs are English Chippendale.

In a city known for its endless social season, there is nothing to compare to the whirl of Mardi Gras, the carnival time that begins shortly after Christmas and lasts until Ash Wednesday: Mardi Gras offers a last indulgence before Lent. The season's revelry was brought to New Orleans by the French, and as the city grew so did the bacchanalian quality of each winter's round of parades and parties. A visitor to New Orleans noted in his journal that his Creole hosts "during a single [season]…execute[d] as much dancing, music, laughing, and dissipation as would serve any reasonably dis-

A silver coffee service for an evening entertainment is set out on the eighteenth-century mahogany sideboard. Fancy pots, cream pitchers, and sugar bowls—of silver or porcelain—were special treasures in a society that made a ritual of serving chicory coffee.

posed, sated, and sober citizens for three or four years." Americans gradually expanded the European customs of Mardi Gras by creating secret societies called krewes ("crews" with a deliberately archaic spelling). The first of these was the Mystic Krewe of Comus, named for a minor Roman god, and through the nineteenth century others flourished: next came the krewes of Rex, Momus, Oberon, Proteus, and Electra. Every year members of krewes elected kings and queens and presented their royal courts in public pageants and at masked balls. While the parades were for anyone who lined the streets, the balls were exclusive; people were known to steal invitations to the more select affairs at the French Opera House and the Théâtre d'Orléans. These were occasions to show off gowns, costumes, and masks from Paris, and the glamor of the guests was legendary. A local society columnist reported during one carnival season: "The six balls held on successive Fridays…presented a gracious blend of beauty, good taste and decorum.

Opposite: Painted herons, nesting in a beautiful swamp area (not far from New Orleans), frame the dining room fireplace—the naturalistic scene is a surprise in a room that is otherwise so restrained. The tiles are original to the house, suggesting that Joseph Maddox found Louisiana's wildlife beautiful.

Overleaf: With crystal, gilt, and silk, the ballroom provides an unexpected display of opulence behind the sober facade of the Maddox-Brennan house. The Corinthian columns support a ceiling hand painted to resemble tapestry. The oak floorboards are laid diagonally, deepening the room.

The allure of our ladies owes little to the glitter of gold, sapphires, emeralds or diamonds. It is due rather to the diaphanous stuff of their gowns, the clinging tulle that sets off their slender figures.... In our spacious, richly ornamented ballrooms where the glitter of a thousand candles is multiplied a thousandfold by mirrors, two hundred young beauties rival each other for grace, elegance, vivacity and youthful ardour." The most social gentleman might augment his krewe activities with a more private soiree—this certainly seems to have been what Maddox had in mind with his ballroom. The Mardi Gras tradition continues in New Orleans—the balls and parades with their elaborate tableaux are a year in the making—and the Maddox-Brennan ballroom is ready to receive guests.

The ballroom, designed to make one gasp, is the most public aspect of the interior of the Maddox-Brennan residence and things take a more intimate turn upstairs. The three bedrooms and one study on the second floor are notable for their size—each is twenty-two feet square with fifteen-foot ceilings. The loftiness is appreciated on still summer days, and the space accommodates the bedroom furnishings, which would seem out of proportion in rooms any smaller: here are monumental tester beds and armoires fashioned in a high rococo style by New Orleanian Prudent Mallard. The rooms are smaller on the half floor above this one, once reserved for children.

Maddox possessed lavish furnishings and all the right appointments. According to his inventory there were several gilt-framed engravings and mirrors, velvet carpeting, curtains of damask and lace, fine pieces of porcelain, yards of tapestry, golden candelabra. There was also a grand piano, most likely in the ballroom. Other fixings included marble-topped side tables of mahogany, an oak sideboard, a suite of mahogany sofas and chairs (upholstered in brocatelle), étagères of oak and mahogany, leather-bottomed chairs, lamps of crystal and brass, and an ivory chess set. Maddox built an enormous house, even by New Orleans standards—the rooms numbered thirty before the *garçonnière* was razed, and the tight urban site made the house seem even larger, as if it had been moved from some plantation on the Mississippi.

A Moorish ceramic figure, on a golden pedestal in the ballroom, could be a reveler at a Mardi Gras costume affair; the bust on the mantel represents another exotically dressed guest. Brass and silver details trim the fireplace (one of two) of black Italian marble and tiles.

There was nothing casual about the location of Maddox's house, for those who built in the Garden District were concerned with the status of address; "Prytania Street" had a particularly nice ring to it, one that matched the architectural message of the house. If the Maddox-Brennan colonnade pays homage to the ideals of classical Greece, so does the name of the street: "Prytania" derives from the Greek *prytanium*, meaning "university," and it was one of several designations in uptown New Orleans striving for Athenian connections. With their imposing Greek Revival houses, men like Joseph Maddox managed to convey two very different things—the democratic aspirations of a young nation, and the powerful aristocracy of the South. The Americans continued to come to New Orleans through the 1870s, building houses in the majestic classical modes. (New Orleans had been fortunate in the Civil War to be only occupied—unlike Atlanta, which was virtually destroyed—and the city prospered long after the Confederacy had ceased to exist.) As the Greek and Gothic revivals waned, Italianate architecture came into vogue, with great blocklike Tuscan villas going up in the Garden District and on Esplanade Avenue downtown. The Creoles and Americans were now having more to do with one another—they had, after all, been conquered as one, which did much to foster bonds between the two peoples. The Vieux Carré ceased to be the exclusive domain of Creoles, though even today there is the occasional elder of French or Spanish descent who will claim never to have ventured across Canal Street. The Vieux Carré and the Garden District keep alive the architectural past, and when visitors tour New Orleans they sense that they are moving between two different worlds, one European, the other American. The distinctions between the parts of town are softened, though, by all the airy, elegant houses, with their cool green gardens and shutters and swirls of iron: they unite the city and identify it unmistakably as New Orleans.

Glass curtains cast lacy shadows onto the dance floor and a sideline chair; in keeping with its surroundings, the chair is gilded. The windows of the ballroom can be raised high, like others in the house—guests could escape the crowd by stepping through the curtains to the side yard or porch.

Acknowledgments

The Editors are particularly grateful to the following people for their extensive assistance and cooperation: Mary Louise Benson, executive secretary, New Orleans Spring Fiesta Association; Timothy J. Chester, chief curator, Louisiana State Museum; Ann M. Masson, director, Gallier House; Vaughn Murmurian; Ann D. Rossi, administrator, Hermann-Grima House.

The Editors would also like to thank the following for their assistance: Mrs. Meryl Aaron; Pamela Arceneaux, reference librarian, The Historic New Orleans Collection; Oscar Lee Bates, Louisiana State Museum; Mrs. Beauregard Bassich; Carolyn Bercier, assistant director, Gallier House; C.J. Blanda; Jan Bradford, curator, Hermann-Grima House; Mrs. Ella Brennan, Maddox-Brennan House; Mary Louise Christovich; Dr. Eugene D. Cizek; Susan Cole, manuscripts curator, The Historic New Orleans Collection; Anne Crounse; Mr. and Mrs. James D. Didier; Jeanette D. Downing, librarian, New Orleans Museum of Art; Sally Kittredge Evans; William Fagalay, assistant director, New Orleans Museum of Art; Thomas Favrot; Rosemarie Fowler; Stanton Frazar, director, The Historic New Orleans Collection; Dr. Edward Haas, director, Louisiana Historical Center, Louisiana State Museum; Mrs. Harley Howcott; Diane Kern, director, Pitot House; Henry Krotzer; Mrs. F. Monroe Labouisse, Jr.; Mrs. Edward F. LeBreton, Jr.; Daniel B. Le Gardeur; Robert R. Macdonald, director, Louisiana State Museum; Charles Mackie, director of public relations, Gallier House; Victor McGee; Patricia McWhorter, assistant curator, The Historic New Orleans Collection; Mrs. Alma Neal, director, Beauregard-Keyes House; Dan Piersol, registrar, New Orleans Museum of Art; Henry Pitot; Dolores Argy Plakotos; Dode Platou, chief curator, The Historic New Orleans Collection; Gary Plum, Louisiana State Museum; Jessie Poesch; Margaret Weese Riley, director of museum sales, Gallier House; Dr. Patricia Brady Schmit, director of publications, The Historic New Orleans Collection; Rodney Smith, Soniat House; Dr. Frederick Starr; Mr. and Mrs. Frank G. Strachan, Strachan House; Roulhac Toledano; Mrs. Genevieve Trimble; Marc Turk, Soniat House; Christina Vella.

Credits

Karchmer. 146: Barbara S. Harvey, Garden Study Club of New Orleans. 147: Paul Rocheleau. 148–151: Barbara S. Harvey, Garden Study Club of New Orleans. 152–153. Pierre De La Barre. 155: Paul Rocheleau. 161: The Historic New Orleans Collection. All other photos are by Karen Radkai.

Index

Page numbers set in *italic* refer to captions.